GW00631019

SPANISH
for Business

Lorna White

Hugo's Language Books Limited

'Spanish for Business' is also available in a pack
with four cassettes: ISBN 0 85285 208 8

Written by

Lorna White

Senior Lecturer in Spanish
South Bank University, London

Edited by
Jenny Yoboué

Cover photo (Robert Harding): Industrial Park of Spain (Barcelona)

Set in Helvetica by
Keyset Composition, Colchester, Essex
Printed and bound in Great Britain by
Page Brothers, Norwich, Norfolk

PREFACE

'Spanish for Business' is one of Hugo's latest language courses specially designed for business and professional people – particularly those wishing to take advantage of new opportunities not only in Europe but also in Latin America. The book is not solely applicable to British users, but will greatly aid any English-speaking person needing to learn Spanish for business purposes. Although this course book is closely modelled on its stable companions 'French for Business' and 'German for Business', it is by no means a carbon copy of these titles. Some of the topics are omitted, or replaced by others more relevant to the Spanish context. We assume that most readers of 'Spanish for Business' have little or a rusty knowledge of Spanish, so we devote quite considerable time to essential basic points of grammar. We think that once you have completed the Course, you should be able to deal with a wide range of business situations linguistically, particularly if you also use the audio-cassettes which are an optional 'extra' to the book. The recorded unit dialogues and exercises provide an additional dimension to your studies and greatly enhance the learning process.

This course is intended for:

a) students who wish to pursue a programme of self-study in business Spanish;
b) readers of our 'Spanish in Three Months' course who now require the language specifically for business or professional reasons;
c) those who studied Spanish some while ago and now need to revise their knowledge thoroughly while continuing their studies in a business context;
d) students for whom Spanish is one of the options on a Business Studies course in colleges or universities.

Whether or not you are an absolute beginner, whether you use 'Spanish for Business' as a self-study programme or in a class, we think you'll find the course enjoyable, fast-moving and methodical.

Method

The method adopted is a very practical one with the emphasis being placed on communication in a realistic context. Every business dialogue in Spanish is accompanied by an English translation, followed by a study of the individual words used (the Checklist), detailed explanatory notes (Checknotes) and abundant examples of grammar 'in action'. Throughout the Course there are numerous varied, lively and contextualized exercises, all with key, offering ample scope for practising what you have been taught. Answers to these exercises are given at the back of the book. Most units include actual, up-to-date Spanish articles (advertisements, telexes, letters etc.) which help explain teaching points and add authenticity and challenge to the exercises.

Theme of the Units

The majority of the units are centred around the activities of a British businessman, Peter Jackson, and his Spanish counterpart, señorita Martín, and cover a wide range of business situations (see Contents). It should be noted however that, with the exception of the authentic material, the names of all persons and companies mentioned in the Course are purely fictitious.

Cassettes

In addition to the chapter devoted to pronunciation, the first three units have been provided with the Hugo system of imitated pronunciation because we feel it is essential for the student to acquire the correct accent from the outset. Nevertheless, we strongly recommend that you obtain the four audio-cassettes which accompany the Course, as these will make the lessons so much more interesting and entertaining and will, of course, accustom your ear to Spanish as pronounced by native speakers.

We hope you will enjoy 'Spanish for Business' and we wish you every success in your studies.

ACKNOWLEDGEMENTS

I am very grateful to Blanca Sálio and Lola Galache for their help in the preparation of this Course, and to Ron Overy for all his advice and suggestions.

CONTENTS

6

The Pronunciation of Spanish

You will be pleased to hear that Spanish is a more phonetic language than English and it is therefore relatively easy to learn how to pronounce it; once you are familiar with the sounds you will know how to pronounce the written word. We have, however, transcribed the opening dialogues in Units 1 to 3 into Hugo's 'imitated pronunciation' to help you get used to the way Spanish is pronounced. Please bear in mind that these descriptions based on Standard British English are merely approximate to the Spanish sounds. You can, if you wish, turn immediately to Unit 1 and begin the first lesson. Alternatively, you may find it useful to read the following general rules fairly rapidly, and refer back to them as you proceed through the Course. If you have obtained the cassettes, so much the better, as you will be able to listen to perfect pronunciation whenever you wish. But, first, make yourself familiar with a few, simple comments regarding the imitated pronunciation.

Imitated Pronunciation

We must, again, emphasize that any system of imitated pronunciation can only be an approximation to the actual sounds and we recommend that you acquire the cassettes which accompany this course. Nevertheless, if you pronounce all the syllables together as if they were a part of an English word, you should have no problem making yourself understood. Before you begin, note the following:

ah	sounds like 'a' in 'father' but shorter.
ai	sounds like 'ai' in 'fair'.
oh	sounds like 'o' in 'local'.
th	sounds like 'th' in 'thin'.
H	sounds like 'ch' in the Scottish word 'loch'.
y	sounds like 'y' in 'yes'.
g	always sounds like 'g' in 'go'.

Stress is indicated by an accent placed above the stressed syllable, for example **tén-goh**; where the syllable is represented by two vowels, we've put the accent over the first only, for example **óo-nah**.

Vowels

The Spanish vowels are **a**, **e**, **i**, **o** and **u**. They are generally shorter and clearer than English vowels.

a   sounds like English 'ah' as in 'father':
     casa ('house') káh-sah

e   (when ending a syllable) sounds like ay in 'say':
     adelante ('come in') ah-day-láhn-tay

e   (when followed by a consonant in the same syllable) sounds like 'e' as in 'let':
     tengo ('I have') tén-goh

i   sounds like 'ee' in 'meet':
     aquí ('here') ah-kée

o   (when ending a syllable) sounds like 'oh' in 'local':
     despacho ('office') dess-páh-choh

o   (when followed by a consonant in the same syllable) sounds like 'o' in 'not':
     once ('eleven') ón-thay

u   sounds like oo as in 'rule':
     su ('his') soo
     silent after 'q':
     quince ('fifteen') kéen-thay
     silent in combinations 'gue' and 'gui':
     guía ('guide') gée-ah
     guerra ('war') gáir-rah

ü   (in combinations 'güe' and 'güi') sounds like 'w' as in 'wet' or 'we':
     bilingüe ('bilingual') bee-léen-gway
     lingüista ('linguist') leen-gwées-tah

Diphthongs

ai ay   sound like 'i' in 'night':
         hay ('there is') 'I'

au   sounds like 'ow' in 'now':
         autobús ('bus') ow-toh-bóoss

ei ey   sound like 'ey' in 'prey':
         veinte ('twenty') báy'n-tay

oi oy	sound almost like 'oy' in 'boy': **hoy** ('today') oy
ui uy	sound like 'we': **muy** ('very') mwee

i	before another vowel sounds like 'y' in 'yes': **Francia** ('France') Fráhn-thyah **principio** ('principle') preen-thée-pyoh
u	before another vowel sounds like 'w' in 'well' **cuatro** ('four') kwáh-troh **puesto** ('job') pwéss-toh

When other combinations of vowels occur, the parts are considered as two distinct syllables:

deuda	('debt') day-óo-dah
creo	('I believe') kráy-oh

Consonants

Most of the Spanish consonants are pronounced more or less in the same way as their English equivalents, but in general more softly. There are, however, ones which you will need to learn since they are pronounced quite differently:

b	sounds like 'b' in 'amber': **banco** ('bank') báhn-koh
c	(before an 'e' or 'i') sounds like 'th' in 'think': **cita** ('appointment') thée-tah **once** ('eleven') ón-thay
c	(on all other occasions) sounds like 'k' in 'cat': **con** ('with') kon **café** ('coffee') kah-fáy
ch	sounds like 'ch' in 'cheap': **mucho** ('much') móo-choh
d	sounds like 'd' in 'day': **despacho** ('office') dess-páh-choh (between vowels and after 'r') sounds almost like 'th' in 'those': **tarde** ('late') táhr-dthay (at the ends of words) the sound can become even more relaxed: **Madrid** Mah-dréedth

f   sounds like 'f' in 'fine':
    fábrica ('factory') fáh-bree-kah

g   (before an 'e' or 'i') sounds like 'ch' in the Scottish word
    'loch':
    general ('general') Hay-nay-ráhl
    (on all other occasions) sounds like 'g' in 'gate':
    algo ('anything') áhl-goh

h   is silent

j   sounds like 'ch' in the Scottish word 'loch':
    trabajo ('work') trah-báh-Hoh

k   sounds like 'k' in 'king':
    kilo kée-loh

l   sounds like 'l' in 'lady':
    planta ('floor', 'storey') pláhn-tah

ll sounds like 'y' in 'yes' (or like 'lli' in 'million' in some parts of
    Spain):
    calle ('street') káh-yay or káh-lyay

m   sounds like 'm' in 'mask':
    mi ('my') mee

n   sounds like 'n' in 'nose'
    un ('a') oon
    (before a written 'v') sounds like 'm' in 'mask':
    enviar ('to send') em-byáhrr

ñ   sounds like 'ny' in 'canyon':
    año ('year') áhn-yoh

p   sounds like 'p' in 'pencil':
    España ('Spain') Ess-páhn-yah

q(u) sounds like 'c' in 'cat':
    ¿qué? ('what?') ¿kay?

r   is always pronounced more strongly than in English.
    caro ('expensive') káhr-oh
    (at the beginning of a word) is strongly rolled:
    reino ('kingdom') rráy-i-noh

rr is very strongly rolled:
    correos ('post office') korr-áy-ohs

s   sounds like 's' in 'simple'
    esto ('this') éss-toh

t   sounds like 't' in 'table':
    tamaño ('size') tah-máhn-yoh

v   sounds like 'b' in 'bath':
    venta ('sale') bén-tah

w   can sound like Spanish 'b' or 'v', or English 'v' or 'w':
      wáter ('lavatory') báh-tairr
      windsurf ('windsurfing') wéen-soorrf

x   (between vowels) sounds like 'gs' in 'tags' or 'ks' in 'box':
      exacto ('exact') eg-sáhk'toh
      taxi ('taxi') táhk-see
      (before a consonant) sounds like 's' in 'soon':
      exportar ('to export') ess-porr-táhrr

y   (between vowels) sounds like 'y' in 'yes'
      mayo ('May') máh-yoh
      (alone) sounds like 'ee' in 'see':
      y ('and') ee

z   sounds like 'th' in 'think':
      luz ('light') looth

Stress

Spanish has fairly simple rules about accentuating words, which
will help you to put the correct stress on a word very quickly:

a) in words which end in a vowel, 'n' or 's', the second to last
    syllable is stressed, for example: c<u>a</u>rta, neces<u>i</u>tan,
    represent<u>a</u>ntes.
b) in words which end in a consonant other than 'n' or 's', the last
    syllable is stressed, for example: Madr<u>i</u>d, españ<u>o</u>l, export<u>a</u>r.
c) in words which are to be stressed contrary to rules a) and b), a
    written accent is required on the stressed syllable, for example:
    ingl<u>é</u>s, representaci<u>ó</u>n, compañ<u>í</u>a, f<u>á</u>brica.
d) the written accent is also used to distinguish some words which
    have the same spelling but different meanings, for example: **el**
    ('the') **él** ('he'), **si** ('if') **sí** ('yes').
e) the vowels 'a', 'e' and 'o' are strong vowels; 'u' and 'i' are weak
    vowels.

    When two strong vowels come together, they are pronounced
    as separate syllables: po<u>e</u>ta ('poet'), te<u>a</u>tro ('theatre'). When two
    weak vowels come together, whilst the second is dominant,
    they form one syllable (i.e. a diphthong): suizo ('Swiss'), viuda
    ('widow').
    When a strong and a weak vowel come together (i.e. a
    diphthong), the strong one is stressed: p<u>ue</u>sto ('job'), fi<u>e</u>sta
    ('party'). In some words, it is the weak vowel which is to be
    stressed and so a written accent is required: per<u>i</u>odo ('period'),
    compañia ('company').

f) Question words bear an accent: ¿**dónde?** ('where?') ¿**qué?** ('what?') ¿**quién?** ('who?').

Punctuation signs

In Spanish, exclamation and question marks are placed both at the beginning and the end of a sentence, but the first one is inverted (¡ and ¿).

The Spanish Alphabet

This differs from English in that there are 29 letters. **Ch, ll** and **ñ** are letters in Spanish, and words beginning with these letters will be found after **c, l** and **n** in Spanish dictionaries. **K** and **w** are found in words taken from other languages. You may well need to know how to spell in Spanish so it is important that you are able to pronounce the letters of the Spanish alphabet. They sound like this:

a	ah	n	énn-ay
b	bay	ñ	énn-yay
c	thay	o	o
ch	chay	p	pay
d	day	q	koo
e	ay	r	áirr-ay
f	éff-ay	s	éss-ay
g	Hay	t	tay
h	áh-chay	u	oo
i	ee	v	óo-bay
j	Hó-tah	w	óo-bay dó-blay
k	kah	x	áy-keess
l	éll-ay	y	ee gryáy-gah
ll	éll-yay	z	thay-tah
m	émm-ay		

At the reception desk

> If you have the audio cassettes, try listening to the dialogue in this unit several times before looking at the text. Then, study this Spanish conversation for a few minutes before comparing it with the English translation which follows. To begin with, you only need to have a general idea of the meaning.
>
> Mr Jackson, a British businessman, has arranged to see señorita Martín of a company called Ecofisa in Madrid. He goes up to the reception desk.

Recepcionista: ¡Buenos días! ¿En qué puedo servirle?

Mr Jackson: ¡Buenos días! Tengo una cita con la señorita Martín.

Recepcionista: ¿De parte de quién, por favor?

Mr Jackson: Del señor Peter Jackson, de la compañía británica Excel-Equip. Aquí tiene mi tarjeta.

Recepcionista: Un momento por favor. ¿Quiere sentarse?

(The receptionist phones through to señorita Martín's secretary)

Recepcionista: Señor Jackson, la secretaria de la señorita Martín está con usted enseguida. Su despacho está en la segunda planta.

Mr Jackson: Muchas gracias.

TRANSLATION

Receptionist: Good morning. (*literally* 'Good days'). How can I help you? (*lit.* 'in what can I serve you?')

Mr Jackson: Good morning. I have an appointment with Miss Martin.

Receptionist: Who shall I say it is? (*lit.* 'on behalf of whom please?')

Mr Jackson: Mr Jackson from the British company Excel-Equip. Here's (*lit.* 'here you have') my card.

> *Receptionist:* Just a moment, please. Would you like to take a seat? (*lit.* 'to sit down?')

(The receptionist phones through to señorita Martín's secretary)

> *Receptionist:* Miss Martin's secretary will be (*lit.* 'is') with you right away. Her office is on the second floor.

> *Mr Jackson:* Thank you very much. (*lit.* 'Many thanks.')

Imitated Pronunciation: If you don't have the cassettes which accompany 'Spanish for Business', and you'd like help with the pronunciation of the dialogues in Units 1–3, turn to the Imitated Pronunciation section at the back of the book.

Checklist 1

Expressions:

¿En qué puedo servirle?	How can I help you?
¿De parte de quién?	Who shall I say it is ... /is calling?
¿Quiere sentarse?	Would you like to sit down?
por favor	please
buenos días	good morning
muchas gracias	thank you very much

Articles:

el	the (masculine singular)
la	the (feminine singular)
un	a, an (masculine)
una	a, an (feminine)

Masculine nouns:

el despacho	the office
el día	the day
el momento	the moment
el señor	the man, gentleman
(el) señor ...	Mr ...

Feminine nouns:

la cita	the appointment
la compañía	the company
la planta	the floor
la recepcionista	the receptionist
la secretaria	the secretary
la señorita	the young lady

(la) señorita ...	Miss ...
la tarjeta	the card

Possessive adjectives:

mi	my
su	her

Personal pronoun:

usted	you (polite)

Interrogative pronoun:

¿qué?	what?

Adjectives:

segundo	second
británico	British

Adverbs:

aquí	here
enseguida	right away, at once, immediately

Verbs:

estar	to be
tener	to have

Prepositions:

con	with
de	of
del = de + el	of the
en	in/on

CHECKNOTES

1 Gender of Spanish nouns

Spanish nouns are either masculine or feminine. Most masculine nouns, but not all, end in -o. Most nouns ending in -a, -ión, -d and -z are feminine. There are, of course, exceptions. You will already have spotted that **día** is masculine.

2 Spanish articles

Articles ('a', 'an', 'the') agree in gender with the noun to which they relate. Here are some examples:

el despacho	the office (*m.*)
la cita	the appointment (*f.*)
un señor	a man (*m.*)
una planta	a floor (*f.*)

3 Greetings

As well as **buenos días** ('good morning'), you'll also need to know **buenas tardes** ('good afternoon/evening') and **buenas noches** ('good evening/night').

4 Spanish subject pronouns

Singular

yo	I
tú	you (familiar)
él, ella	he, she
usted (Vd.)	you (polite)

Plural

nosotros (*m.*) **nosotras** (*f.*)	we
vosotros (*m.*) **vosotras** (*f.*)	you (*fam.*)
ellos (*m.*) **ellas** (*f.*)	they
ustedes (Vds.)	you (*pol.*)

5 Personal pronoun 'You'

There are four forms for YOU in Spanish.
Strictly speaking, the forms **tú** and **vosotros/as** (familiar forms) are used to address members of the family, friends, children and

animals. The forms **usted** and **ustedes** (polite forms) are used to address all other people; often written as **Vd.** and **Vds.** in Spain, and as **Ud.** and **Uds.** in Latin America. Although the familiar form is being increasingly used in Spain, it is advisable to keep to **Vd./Vds.** – the polite form – when talking to people you don't know or have just met, and in formal situations. You'll have noticed that in the conversation the polite form – **usted** – is used.

6 Using the subject pronoun

In Spanish you can usually leave out the subject pronoun when you use it with a verb, unless you want to emphasize the person i.e. He is in Madrid – **él está en Madrid**, *she* is in Valencia – **ella está en Valencia**. To avoid ambiguity, **Vd.** and **Vds.** are nearly always expressed.

7 The verb **estar** ('to be')

It's an irregular verb – i.e. the various parts of it don't follow a clear-cut pattern – so learn it carefully. As shown in the Checklist, **está** means 'is'; the rest of the present tense is as follows:

estoy	I am
estás	you are (*fam. sing.*)
está	he, she, it is
	you are (*pol. sing.*)
estamos	we are
estáis	you are (*fam. pl.*)
están	they are
	you are (*pol. pl.*)

8 The verb **tener** ('to have')

This is another important verb which is also irregular. You'll have met **tengo** and **tiene** in the dialogue; here is the rest of the present tense:

tengo	I have
tienes	you have (*fam. sing.*)
tiene	he/she/it has
	you have (*pol. sing.*)

tenemos	we have
tenéis	you have (*fam. pl.*)
tienen	they have
	you have (*pol. pl.*)

9 Adjectives

Most, though not all, adjectives are placed AFTER the noun they describe, i.e. 'British company' becomes 'company British' – **compañía británica**. Note also that adjectives of nationality don't take a capital letter.

A further rule is that adjectives need to agree in gender (masculine or feminine) and number (singular or plural) with the noun they describe.

Adjectives ending in **-o** are masculine. Change the **-o** to **-a** to make them feminine. And just add an **-s** to make them plural.

Examples:

una secretaria británica	a British secretary
una compañía norteamericana	an American company

BUT, note that ordinal numbers normally go before the noun:

la segunda cita	the second appointment

10 The plural

Just add **-s** to nouns ending in a vowel, and **-es** to nouns ending in a consonant:

cita (appointment)	→	**citas** (appointments)
señor (man)	→	**señores** (men)

The plural of articles:

los the (*m.*)	**unos** some (*m.*)
las the (*f.*)	**unas** some (*f.*)

Comprehension Practice 1

Re-read or listen again to the conversation between the reception-
ist and Mr Jackson at the beginning of this unit, and then say
*whether the following statements are true **(verdadero)** or false*
(falso). *Before you begin, look at the following:*

New words:

la recepción	the reception	**italiano**	Italian
norteamericano	American	**cuarto**	fourth
Londres	London	**España**	Spain
Nueva York	New York	**(la) señora**	Mrs...

1 El señor Jackson está en Madrid.	verdadero/falso
2 Tiene una cita con el señor Martín.	verdadero/falso
3 El despacho de la señorita Martín está en la segunda planta.	verdadero/falso
4 La secretaria está en la recepción.	verdadero/falso
5 La señorita Martín tiene una secretaria italiana.	verdadero/falso
6 La recepción está en la cuarta planta.	verdadero/falso

FLUENCY PRACTICE 1

Arriving at reception

Look at or listen to the conversation again and then take part in this short dialogue:

You:	(Say good morning and say you have an appointment with Miss Martín.)
Recepcionista:	**¿De parte de quién, por favor?**
You:	(Say your name.)
Recepcionista:	**Un momento, por favor. ¿Quiere sentarse?**
You:	(Thank her!)

Now, using some of the new words, take part in this conversation:

You:	(Say good afternoon, and say you have an appointment with Mrs Martin.)

Recepcionista:	¿De parte de quién, por favor?
You:	(Tell her your name and say that you are from the American company Equip.)
Recepcionista:	Un momento, por favor. ¿Quiere sentarse?
You:	(Thank her!)

FLUENCY PRACTICE 2

In this exercise, make sentences using the correct part of the verb **estar** ('to be'). Say them aloud, if possible, trying to concentrate on good pronunciation. Consult the Key at the back of the book if you need help.

Example: **Su despacho está en la segunda planta.**
His office is on the second floor.

Now make similar sentences using different words:

el señor Jackson	la recepción
yo	mi despacho
nosotros	Madrid
los señores	Nueva York
ustedes	la cuarta planta
la secretaria	Londres

FLUENCY PRACTICE 3

Can you change the following into the plural?

el señor
un despacho
la señorita italiana
tengo una cita
la compañía tiene una recepcionista británica

FLUENCY PRACTICE 4

Using the verb **tener**, can you say . . .

She's got an appointment.
I've an office on the fourth floor.
The receptionist has my card.
You have an Italian secretary. (use **tú**)
We have a company in New York.

ECOFISA   **Equipos de Oficina, S.A.**

Mercedes Martín Delgado
Director
Publicidad y Márketing

Maura 25, 1.º izqda.   *Teléfs 435-67-89 435-32-10*
28115 Alcobendas   *Fax 566-77 22*

TARJETA DE LA SRTA MARTÍN

You'll notice that Mercedes Martín has two surnames. The Spanish keep the surnames of both parents. Martín is Mercedes' father's surname, and Delgado her mother's. If Mercedes were to marry, for example, a señor Escudero, she would call herself Mercedes Martín de Escudero. A son called Juan would be Juan Escudero Martín.

Introducing yourself

> *Again, if you have the audio cassettes, it's a good idea to listen to the dialogue in this unit several times before looking at the Spanish text.*

Señorita Martín's secretary has now arrived at the reception desk.

Mr Jackson:	¡Buenos días!
Secretaria:	Hola. ¡Buenos días! Soy María López, la secretaria de la señorita Martín. ¿Es Vd. el señor Jackson?
Mr Jackson:	Sí. Tengo una cita con la señorita Martín a las once.
Secretaria:	Ah sí. Le espera en su despacho. ¿Me acompaña, por favor?

(The secretary takes Mr Jackson up to señorita Martín's office, and knocks on the door ...)

Señorita Martín:	Sí. Adelante.
Secretaria:	Señorita Martín, el señor Jackson está aquí.
Señorita Martín:	¡Ah! ¿Son las once ya? ¡Bienvenido a Madrid, señor Jackson!

(They shake hands)

Mr Jackson:	Gracias. Encantado de conocerla.
Señorita Martín:	Siéntese, por favor. ¿Quiere tomar algo?
Mr Jackson:	Un té, muchas gracias.
Señorita Martín:	Por favor, María, un té para el señor Jackson y ... yo voy a tomar un café. Bueno, ¿y qué tal su viaje ...?

TRANSLATION

Mr Jackson:	Good morning!
Secretary:	Hello, good morning. I am María López, Miss Martín's secretary (*lit.* the secretary of Miss Martín). Are you Mr Jackson?
Mr Jackson:	Yes. I have an appointment with Miss Martín at 11 o'clock.
Secretary:	Ah, yes. She is expecting you (*lit.* you expects) in her office. Will you come with me, please? (*lit.* me accompany please).

(The secretary takes Mr Jackson up to señorita Martín's office and knocks on the door.)

Señorita Martín:	Yes. Come in.
Secretary:	Miss Martín, Mr Jackson is here.
Señorita Martín:	Ah! Is it 11 o'clock already? Welcome to Madrid, Mr Jackson!

(They shake hands)

Mr Jackson:	Thank you. How do you do. (*lit.* Pleased to meet you.)
Señorita Martín:	Do sit down, please. Would you like to have something (to drink)?
Mr Jackson:	A tea, thank you.
Señorita Martín:	Please, María, a tea for Mr Jackson, and . . . I'll (*lit.* I'm going to) have a coffee. Right. And how was your journey?

Checklist 2

Expressions:

adelante	come in
bienvenido -a (*f.*)	welcome
bueno	right
sí	yes
hola	hello
siéntese	do sit down (polite)
a las once	at eleven o'clock
son las once	it's eleven o'clock
voy a . . .	I'm going to . . .
¿quiere . . .?	Would you like . . .?

¿qué tal?	How was/is …?
encantado -a (*f.*)	pleased to meet you (*m./f.*)
de conocerla -le (*m.*)	

Masculine nouns:

un café	a coffee
un té	a tea
el viaje	the journey

Verbs:

acompañar	to accompany
esperar	to expect
tomar	to take, have (a drink)
ser	to be

Adjectives:

| encantado | pleased, delighted, charmed |
| bienvenido | welcome |

Adverb:

| ya | already |

Object pronouns:

| le | you (masculine) |
| me | me |

Possessive adjective:

| su | her, your, his |

Pronoun:

| algo | something |

Conjunction:

| y | and |

Prepositions:

| a | at (in expressions of time) |
| para | for |

CHECKNOTES

11 The verb 'to be'

You'll have noted that there are two verbs 'to be'. **Estar**, featured in Unit 1, is used to denote the position of something or someone.

Ser is used:
1 to indicate identity

Soy María.	I am María.
Es el señor Jackson.	It/He is Mr Jackson.

2 to indicate occupation

María es la recepcionista.	Mary is the receptionist.

3 to indicate nationality

Somos británicos.	We are British.

4 in expressions of time

Son las once.	It's eleven o'clock.

Ser is irregular. Here are the other parts of the present tense:

soy	I am
eres	you are (*fam. sing.*)
es	he/she/it is,
	you are (*pol. sing.*)
somos	we are
sois	you are (*fam. pl.*)
son	they are
	you are (*pol. pl.*)

12 Verbs ending in -AR

In Spanish dictionaries, there are many thousands of verbs ending in -AR which is the equivalent of the English 'to'. Here are some examples:

acompañar	to accompany, go/come with
pasar	to pass, spend (time)
hablar	to speak
tomar	to take/have (a drink)
esperar	to expect, wait for
bajar	to go/come down

The present tense of **-AR** verbs

This is how verbs ending in **-AR** perform in the present tense. Most verbs follow this pattern so it's worthwhile learning it thoroughly now. The endings are underlined:

hablar	'to speak'
hablo	I speak
hablas	you speak (*fam. sing.*)
habla	he/she/it speaks
	you speak (*pol. sing.*)
hablamos	we speak
habláis	you speak (*fam. pl.*)
hablan	they speak
	you speak (*pol. pl.*)

13 The possessive

The possessive apostrophe 's' ('s) which we use in English doesn't exist in Spanish. So, instead of saying 'Mary's office', you have to say 'the office of Mary' – **el despacho de María**. Similarly, 'Mr Jackson's card' is rendered in Spanish as **la tarjeta del señor Jackson**.

14 Possessive adjectives

Su means 'his', 'her', 'their' or 'your' when the thing possessed is singular. The plural is **sus**.

su secretaria	her secretary
sus citas	your appointments
sus tarjetas	her cards
su recepcionista	their receptionist
sus viajes	their journeys
su despacho	his office
su compañía	his company

15 Cardinal numbers

0	cero	6	seis
1	uno (*m.*) una (*f.*)	7	siete
2	dos	8	ocho
3	tres	9	nueve
4	cuatro	10	diez
5	cinco	11	once

12	doce	21	veintiuno (*m.*), veintiuna (*f.*)
13	trece	22	veintidós
14	catorce	23	veintitrés
15	quince	24	veinticuatro
16	dieciséis	25	veinticinco
17	diecisiete	26	veintiséis
18	dieciocho	27	veintisiete
19	diecinueve	28	veintiocho
20	veinte	29	veintinueve

'One' and 'twenty-one' change according to the gender of the noun and are shortened before a masculine noun, for example:

Tiene una secretaria.	She has a/one secretary.
Pasan veintiún días en Londres.	They spend 21 days in London.

16 The time

Telling the time is relatively simple, as you can see from the following examples:

es la una	it's one o'clock
son las tres	it's three o'clock
son las diez	it's ten o'clock

The feminine article – **la** (in 'one o'clock') and **las** (in all the other hours) – is inserted before the number.

To ask what the time is you say **¿Qué hora es?**

17 ¿Qué tal?

This is a very handy little phrase which on its own means 'How are things?', 'How are you?' or 'How goes it?'

Used with **estar** – **¿Qué tal estás?**, it means 'How are you?'; used with **ser** – **¿Qué tal es?** it means 'What's (s)he like?' and with nouns – **¿Qué tal la comida?** it means 'How is/was the meal?'

18 Addressing people

Take a look at the dialogue again, and you'll notice that when talking about people formally, Spanish slips in the definite article in front of the title, for example:

<u>la</u> señorita Martín está aquí	Miss Martin is here
<u>el</u> señor Jackson le espera	Mr Jackson is expecting you

Los señores López son españoles.
Mr and Mrs López are Spanish.

When addressing someone directly, however, the article is dropped:

Buenas tardes, señorita Martín. – Good afternoon, Miss Martín.

Note that **señor, señorita, señora** don't require a capital 's'. However, when abbreviated, they can be written like this: **Sr, Srta, Sra.**

19 Personal **a**

All verbs except **tener** are followed by the preposition **a** if the direct object is a specific person or group of persons.

Espero a mi secretaria.	I'm expecting my secretary.
Acompañamos a María.	We are accompanying Mary.

20 Al = a + el   del = de + el

When the prepositions 'a' and 'de' are followed by the definite article **el**, they contract into **al** and **del** respectively.

baja al despacho	he goes down to the office
hablan al director	they speak to the director
el despacho del señor Jackson	Mr Jackson's office
la tarjeta del señor	the gentleman's card

Comprehension Practice 2

*Re-read the conversation at the beginning of this unit (or listen to it again on the cassette), note the new words below, and then answer the questions – **verdadero/falso** – true/false.*

New words:

representar a to represent (a company)
una cerveza a beer **el bar** the bar

1 María López es la secretaria de la señorita Martín.
2 El señor Jackson tiene una cita a las diez.
3 La señorita Martín toma un té.
4 La señorita Martín está con el señor Jackson en un bar.
5 María López espera al señor Jackson en su despacho.
6 El señor Jackson acompaña a la secretaria al despacho de la señorita Martín.
7 El señor Jackson representa a una compañía australiana.
8 El señor Jackson toma una cerveza.

FLUENCY PRACTICE 5

Some more new words:

una reunión	a meeting
reservar	to reserve, book
el hotel	the hotel
organizar	to arrange, organize

In the conversation, señorita Martín asks Mr Jackson ¿**Quiere tomar algo?** 'Would you like something (to drink)'. This structure of ¿**quiere + infinitive of the verb** can be used in other situations. Here's an example:

¿**Quiere + hablar con el señor López?**
Would you like + to speak with/to Mr López?

Using the expression ¿**quiere ... plus verb infinitive**, ask a colleague if he/she would like ...

1 to wait in the reception please?
2 to spend the day in Madrid?
3 to represent the company at the meeting?
4 to have a beer?

5 to arrange the appointment with Miss López?
6 to book the hotel?

Colleague: **Muy bien** ('all right')

FLUENCY PRACTICE 6

Similarly, with the expression **voy a + verb infinitive**, you can inform someone of your intentions. Here's an example:

voy a reservar el hotel   I'm going to book the hotel

Tell your secretary that you are going . . .

1 to have a beer.
2 to be in Madrid at 7 o'clock. (Remember to choose the correct verb to be!)
3 to spend ten days in Barcelona.
4 to speak immediately with Mr González.
5 to wait in the reception.
6 to represent the British company in Zaragoza.

Secretary: **Muy bien, señor.** ('All right, sir.')

FLUENCY PRACTICE 7

Some new words:

la ofimática	office automation
el especialista	the specialist
también	also, as well

Imagine you are in Valencia for a meeting with a Spanish agent. You arrive at reception and this is your conversation.

Receptionist: **¡Buenas tardes!**

You: Hello, good afternoon. I am Tom Smith. I have an appointment with Mr González at 5 o'clock.

Receptionist: **Sí, señor. ¿Tiene su tarjeta?**

You: Yes, here it is.

Receptionist: **El señor González le espera. ¿Me acompaña, por favor?**

(You are taken to Mr González's office and shown in)

Mr González: **Buenas tardes y bienvenido a Valencia.**

You: Pleased to meet you. (*Shake hands*)

Mr González: Siéntese aquí por favor. ¿Quiere tomar algo?

You: Yes, a coffee, thank you.

Mr González: Bueno. Vd. representa a la compañía Excel-Equip.

You: Yes, and I also represent two American companies. We are specialists in office automation.

Mr González: Bien. ¡Ah! Su café.

You: Thank you.

FLUENCY PRACTICE 8

Now practise some numbers. Write or, even better, repeat aloud in Spanish the following phrases:

1 7 offices
2 3 Italian secretaries
3 6 coffees
4 4 floors
5 9 days
6 5 British companies
7 8 hotels
8 15 specialists
9 29 bars
10 1 tea
11 20 appointments
12 22 journeys
13 11 beers
14 19 cards

FLUENCY PRACTICE 9

Fill in the gaps with the correct part of the verbs to be – **ser** or **estar**. Look back at Checknotes 7 and 11 for the rules!

1 Yo ... en Londres.
2 María ... la secretaria.
3 Nosotros ... en el despacho del señor Jackson.
4 Voy a ... en Valladolid a las diez.
5 Antonio y María ... americanos.
6 ... las ocho.
7 Excel-Equip ... una compañía británica.
8 ¿ ... Vds. de la compañía Excel-Equip?
9 Vosotros ... en el Hotel Continental.
10 Las señoritas ... recepcionistas en la compañía en Madrid.

FLUENCY PRACTICE 10

Now see if you can use some of the verbs introduced in this unit. They all belong to the **-AR** group, and you may want to look back at the rules and refresh your memory.

Complete the sentences with the correct part of the verb in brackets:

1 Yo (**representar**) a una compañía italiana.
2 El señor (**esperar**) en el hotel.
3 Nosotros (**pasar**) diez días en Madrid.
4 ¿(**organizar**) usted la reunión?
5 Juan y yo (**tomar**) café.
6 Voy a (**pasar**) cinco días en Madrid.
7 Los señores (**hablar**) con la recepcionista.
8 La señorita Martín (**bajar**) a la recepción.
9 ¿(**reservar**) vosotros el hotel?
10 ¿Me (**acompañar**) ustedes a la recepción?

Mr Jackson probably travelled to Spain with British Airways or Iberia, the Spanish national airline. Once there, he may have used the internal airline AVIACO or the rail network RENFE.

LARGO RECORRIDO

Información en RENFE y Agencias de Viajes.

UN BUEN NEGOCIO

*The **Talgo** is an inter-city train, and the **Ave** is the new high-speed train between Madrid and Seville.*

Getting down to business

Study the following dialogue in the usual way.

Coffee and tea have been brought. Now Mr Jackson is invited to talk about his firm and his plans to export office equipment to Spain.

Señorita Martín: Gracias por su carta en la que explican su intención de exportar equipos de oficina a España.

Mr Jackson: Sí, ya vendemos nuestros productos en Francia y Alemania y con la presencia de España en la Unión Europea y las ventajas del Mercado Único, creemos que existen buenas oportunidades en el mercado español.

Señorita Martín: Bueno, señor Jackson, debo decir que no conozco su compañía. Se llama Excel-Equip, ¿verdad?

Mr Jackson: Sí. No somos una compañía del tamaño de una multinacional. Tenemos nuestra sede en Londres y fábricas en otras ciudades del sur de Inglaterra. Somos muy conocidos por todo el Reino Unido ya que llevamos muchos años especializándonos en equipos electrónicos para oficinas. Fabricamos calculadoras, micro-ordenadores, procesadores de textos, terminales de impresoras, máquinas telefax, contestadores automáticos, etcétera, es decir, todo lo que se necesita en una oficina moderna.

Señorita Martín: Observo que son especialistas en tecnología avanzada.

Mr Jackson: Sí, eso es. Por otra parte, tengo entendido que su compañía está especializada en la representación de empresas extranjeras que trabajan en el campo de la ofimática. Estamos buscando a un representante comercial. Éste es el motivo de mi visita a Madrid.

TRANSLATION

Señorita Martín:	Thanks for your letter, in which you explain your intention to export office equipment (*lit.* equipments of office) to Spain.
Mr Jackson:	Yes, we already sell (*lit.* already we sell) our products in France and Germany, and with Spain (*lit.* the presence of Spain) in the European Union (*lit.* Union European) and the advantages of the Single Market (*lit.* Market Single), we believe that good opportunities exist (*lit.* exist good opportunities) in the Spanish market (*lit.* market Spanish).
Señorita Martín:	Well, Mr Jackson, I have to say that I do not know your company. It's called (*lit.* it calls itself) Excel-Equip, isn't it (*lit.* truth)?
Mr Jackson:	Yes. We aren't (*lit.* not we are) as big a company as (*lit.* a company of the size of) a multinational. We have our head office in London and factories in other cities in the (*lit.* of the) south of England. We are very well known (*lit.* known) throughout (*lit.* through all) the United Kingdom (*lit.* Kingdom United) since we have been specializing in electronic equipment for offices for many years. (*lit.* We spend many years specializing ourselves in equipment electronic for offices.) We make calculators, computers, word processors, printer terminals (*lit.* terminals of printers), fax machines, automatic answering machines, (*lit.* answering machines automatic), etc, in other words (*lit.* it's to say) everything (*lit.* all) that (*lit.* that which) is needed (*lit.* one needs) in a modern office (*lit.* office modern).
Señorita Martín:	I see (*lit.* note) that you specialize (*lit.* are specialists) in advanced technology (*lit.* technology advanced).
Mr Jackson:	Yes, that's right. (*lit.* that's so). On the other hand (*lit.* as other side), I gather (*lit.* I have (it) understood) that your company specializes in representing (*lit.* is specialized in the representation of) foreign companies (companies foreign) which work in the field of office automation. We are looking for a business representative. This is the purpose of my visit to Madrid.

Checklist 3

Expressions:

bueno ...	well ...
no	no, not
¿verdad?	isn't it?
llevamos muchos años especializándonos	we have been specializing for many years
es decir	in other words
eso es	that's right
por otra parte	on the other hand
en la que	in which
etcétera	etcetera

Proper names:

Francia	France
Alemania	German
Inglaterra	England
El Reino Unido	the United Kingdom
El Mercado Único	the Single (European) Market
La Comunidad	the Community
La Unión Europea	the European Union
La UE	the EU

Masculine nouns:

el tamaño	the size
el equipo	the piece of equipment, gear, team
los equipos	the equipment
el producto	the product
el mercado	the market
el micro-ordenador	the (micro-)computer
el procesador	the processor
el texto	the text
el procesador de textos	the word processor
el contestador	the answering machine
el (tele)fax	the fax
el campo	the field, area
el motivo	the purpose, reason
el sur	the south
el reino	the kingdom
el año	the year
el representante	the representative

Feminine nouns:

la carta	the letter

la presencia	the presence
la ventaja	the advantage
la comunidad	the community
la oportunidad	the opportunity
la oficina	the office
la verdad	the truth
la ciudad	the city
la sede	the main/head office, headquarters
la fábrica	the factory
la máquina	the machine
la terminal	the terminal
la impresora	the printer
la calculadora	the calculator
la tecnología	the technology
la representación	the representation
la empresa	the company
la visita	the visit
la intención	the intention
la multinacional	the multinational (company)

Verbs:

explicar	to explain
exportar	to export
vender	to sell
creer	to think, believe
existir	to exist
deber	to owe, have to, must
decir	to say
conocer	to know
llamarse	to be called
llevar	to carry, wear
especializarse	to specialize
fabricar	to make, manufacture
necesitar	to need
observar	to observe, note
tener entendido	to understand, gather
buscar	to look for

Adjectives:

único	single, sole, only
europeo	European
español	Spanish
otro	another, other
conocido	(well-) known
todo	all
automático	automatic
moderno	modern

electrónico	electronic
especializado	specialized
avanzado	advanced
extranjero	foreign
unido	united
mucho	much
muchos/as	many
entendido	understood, agreed
comercial	commercial, of trade or business

Possessive adjective:

nuestro	our

Relative pronouns:

que	that, which, who
lo que	what, that which

Conjunction:

ya que	since, as

Prepositions:

por	through(out), by, for
para	for, in order to

Pronoun:

se	it/her/himself, yourself, themselves

Demonstrative pronouns:

eso	that, that matter
éste	this (one)

CHECKNOTES

21 Regular verbs ending in -ER and -IR

The infinitive of every Spanish verb ends in either **-AR** (which you learnt about in Unit 2) or **-ER** or **-IR**. They all have quite distinctive endings to indicate who is doing the action. Here are the patterns for the Present Tense of the -ER and -IR verbs:

vender	'to sell'	**escribir**	'to write'
vendo	I sell	**escribo**	I write
vendes	you sell (*fam. sing.*)	**escribes**	you write
vende	he/she/it sells	**escribe**	he/she/it writes
	you sell (*pol. sing.*)		you write
vendemos	we sell	**escribimos**	we write
vendéis	you sell (*fam. pl.*)	**escribís**	you write
venden	they sell	**escriben**	they write
	you sell (*pol. pl.*)		you write

Here are some regular verbs for reference:

aprender	to learn	**recibir**	to receive
creer	to believe, think	**vivir**	to live
deber	to owe	**decidir**	to decide
comer	to eat	**existir**	to exist
beber	to drink	**abrir**	to open
correr	to run	**subir**	to go up
leer	to read	**asistir**	to be present (attend)
responder	to answer, respond	**admitir**	to admit, accept, recognize

Examples:

Leen el texto.
They read the text.

¿Vives en Londres?
Do you live in London?

Sube a la segunda planta.
He goes up to the second floor.

22 The verb **decir** ('to say, tell')

This verb is irregular in the Present Tense:

digo	I say
dices	you say (*fam. sing.*)

dice	he/she/it says
	you say (*pol. sing.*)
decimos	we say
decís	you say (*fam. pl.*)
dicen	they say
	you say (*pol. pl.*)

Here are some examples:

Digo que fabricamos máquinas muy buenas.
I'm saying that we manufacture very good machines.

¿Decís que estáis buscando al representante?
Are you saying you are looking for the representative?

23 The present participle

The present participle of regular verbs is formed by adding **-ando** to the stem of **-AR** verbs, and **-iendo** to the stem of **-ER** and **-IR** verbs. For example:

hablar → **hablando** ('speaking')
comer → **comiendo** ('eating')
escribir → **escribiendo** ('writing')

24 Present continuous tense

This tense is formed just as it is in English. Use the verb 'to be' **estar** with the present participle (I am speaking, she is eating, we are writing, etc). Its use is more restricted than the English and generally indicates an action taking place at the time of speaking. Regular verbs have the following patterns:

hablar	'to speak'
estoy hablando	I am speaking
estás hablando	you are speaking
está hablando	he/she/it is speaking
	you are speaking
estamos hablando	we are speaking
estáis hablando	you are speaking
están hablando	they are speaking
	you are speaking

Example:

Estoy hablando con el señor Jackson.
I'm speaking with/to Mr Jackson.

comer	'to eat'
estoy comiendo	I am eating
estás comiendo	you are eating
está comiendo	he/she/it is eating
	you are eating
estamos comiendo	we are eating
estáis comiendo	you are eating
están comiendo	they are eating
	you are eating

Example:

Juan está comiendo una hamburguesa en el bar.
John is eating a hamburger in the bar.

escribir	'to write'
estoy escribiendo	I am writing
estás escribiendo	you are writing
está escribiendo	he/she/it is writing
	you are writing
estamos escribiendo	we are writing
estáis escribiendo	you are writing
están escribiendo	they are writing
	you are writing

Example:

Estamos escribiendo una carta.
We're writing a letter.

25 Reflexive verbs

Llamar means 'to call' but **llamarse** means 'to call oneself', 'to be called'. Verbs which have this **se** attached to them are called reflexive verbs. The present tense set out below indicates the words for 'myself', 'himself', etc.

me llamo	I call myself (my name is)
te llamas	you call yourself (your name is)
se llama	he/she/it calls himself/herself/itself (his/her/its name is)
	you call yourself (your name is)
nos llamamos	we call ourselves (our name is)
os llamáis	you call yourselves (your name is)
se llaman	they call themselves (their name is)
	you call yourselves (your name is)

It's easy to see why verbs like **lavarse** ('to wash oneself') and **mirarse** ('to look at oneself') have the **se** attached – it means 'oneself'. Sometimes, however, a verb will be reflexive when you wouldn't have expected it to be so.

For example: **especializarse**   'to specialize'
              levantarse   'to get up'

Nos especializamos en máquinas electrónicas.
We specialize in electronic machines.

As you can see, the pronouns 'myself', 'yourself' etc. normally go before the verb in Spanish. When the present continuous is used or when an infinitive of the verb is involved, you can tag the pronoun on to the end, for example:

me levanto   I get up
voy a levantarme   I'm going to get up
estoy levantándome   I am getting up

(The accent in **levantándome** is there to keep the stress of the verb on the original syllable.)

26 The reflexive pronoun **se**

The reflexive pronoun **se** can also be used when you want to make an impersonal statement. For instance:

Aquí se habla español.   Spanish is spoken here.
Se necesita una oficina moderna.   A modern office is needed.
Se dice que ...   One says/It is said/They say that ...

27 Negative

To make a sentence negative, all you have to do is put **no** in front of the verb. For example:

no comprendo   I don't understand
no vendemos   we don't sell
no fabrican máquinas   they don't make machines

Some other negatives which you will need are: **nunca** 'never', **nada** 'nothing', **nadie** 'nobody'. Simply put **no** before the verb and the negative word after it, like this:

No voy nunca a la fábrica.
I never go to the factory.

No tenemos nada.
We have nothing/We don't have anything.

No hay nadie aquí.
There is nobody here/There isn't anybody here.

28 Adjectives of nationality

Adjectives of nationality ending in a consonant in the masculine, take an '**a**' in the feminine. The plural is formed by adding '**es**' to the masculine and '**s**' to the feminine.

For example:

el mercado español	the Spanish market
productos españoles	Spanish products
una empresa española	a Spanish company
ciudades españolas	Spanish cities

29 The verb **conocer** ('to know')

This verb means 'to be acquainted with', 'to know a person/place'.

Unfortunately, it doesn't follow the regular pattern and slips in a '**z**' before the '**c**' in the first person, but the rest of the tense is regular:

conozco	I know
conoces	you know
conoce	he/she/it knows
	you know
conocemos	we know
conocéis	you know
conocen	they know
	you know

Here are some examples:

Conozco al señor López.	I know Mr López.
No conocemos Madrid.	We don't know Madrid.

30 The verb **llevar**

Llevar normally means 'to wear' or 'to carry'. However, it is often used together with the present participle to express how long something has been going on.

For example:

Llevo dos horas esperando.   I have been waiting two hours.

¿Cuánto tiempo llevas   How long have you been
estudiando español?   studying Spanish?

Llevan un año viviendo en Londres.
They have been living in London a year.

31 Demonstrative adjectives

These go before the noun and always agree in number and gender.

	Masc.	Fem.
this	**este**	**esta**
that	**ese**	**esa**
that (over there)	**aquel**	**aquella**
these	**estos**	**estas**
those	**esos**	**esas**
those (over there)	**aquellos**	**aquellas**

For example:

este mercado	this market
esas empresas	those companies
aquel señor	that man (over there)

32 Demonstrative pronouns

These are just the same as the adjectives, except that they take an accent on the stressed syllable. For example:

No es esta oficina, es aquélla.
It's not this office, but that one over there.

Esta compañía es española, ésa es italiana.
This company is Spanish, that one is Italian.

The neuter forms of the pronoun **esto** ('this') and **eso**, **aquello** ('that') are used to refer to things the gender of which is not known. Note that these forms bear no accent. For example:

¿Qué es esto?	What is this?
Eso no es fácil.	That isn't easy.

33 ¿verdad?

This one little word is equivalent to the English 'isn't it?', 'aren't you?', 'doesn't it', etc. You would use it after you have made a statement and wish to have confirmation that it is right.

For example:

Vives en Londres, ¿verdad?   You live in London, don't you?

Comprehension Practice 3

New word: **comprar**   to buy

¿verdadero o falso?   *true or false?*

1 Excel-Equip tiene la intención de exportar cerveza a España.
2 Ya vende sus productos en España.
3 España está en la Unión Europea.
4 La señorita Martín conoce muy bien la compañía Excel-Equip.
5 La sede de Excel-Equip está en Nueva York.
6 Excel-Equip se especializa en la representación de empresas británicas.
7 El señor Jackson está en Madrid para comprar equipos de oficina.

FLUENCY PRACTICE 11

New words:

la máquina de escribir	the typewriter
la formación	the training
el personal	the staff
la fabricación	the manufacture
la importación	the import, importation

Using the verb **especializarse en** tell your potential customer that you specialize in:

a) the training of staff
b) advanced technology
c) the manufacture of electronic typewriters
d) office automation
e) the importation of American computers

FLUENCY PRACTICE 12

New word: importar   to import

Answer these questions in the same way as the following example, in the person indicated by the pronoun in the brackets:

¿Exporta máquinas a España? (yo)
Do you export machines to Spain?

Sí, exporto máquinas a España.
Yes, I export machines to Spain.

1 ¿Importan ordenadores de Alemania? (**nosotros**)
2 ¿Escribe las cartas la secretaria? (**ella**)
3 ¿Trabajáis en Nueva York? (**nosotros**)
4 ¿Vivís en el sur de España? (**nosotros**)
5 ¿Comen los señores López en el bar? (**ellos**)

FLUENCY PRACTICE 13

New words:

inglés	English
el cliente	the client, customer

Imagine that you have a slight difference of opinion with one of your colleagues. When he/she makes a statement, you disagree, like this:

Representamos a una compañía española.
We represent a Spanish company.

No, no representamos a una compañía española.
No, we don't represent a Spanish company.

1 Llevamos muchos años especializándonos en la ofimática.
2 Su compañía importa productos australianos.
3 Nuestro cliente está buscando a un representante.
4 Fabrica todo lo que se necesita para la oficina moderna.
5 El Mercado Único ofrece muchas ventajas.

FLUENCY PRACTICE 14

New words:

el congreso	the congress, conference, convention
el paquete	the parcel, package, packet
terminar	to finish

Match the words in the first column with those in the second:

a) Ella quiere   f) recibís el paquete.
b) Estoy   g) hablan en español.
c) Vosotros   h) termina a las cinco.
d) La reunión   i) asistir al congreso.
e) La señorita Martín   j) escribiendo una carta.
   y el señor Smith

FLUENCY PRACTICE 15

New word: **el informe**   the report

Replace the infinitives in the brackets with the correct part of the verb:

a) Yo no **(beber)** cerveza.
b) Nosotros **(terminar)** la reunión a las dos.
c) Ella **(llamarse)** María López.
d) El señor González **(hablar)** del informe.
e) Vosotros **(vender)** muchos productos.

FLUENCY PRACTICE 16

Imagine you are in a meeting with el señor González talking about your companies:

Sr González: **Su compañía tiene la intención de exportar ordenadores, ¿verdad?**

You: We already export computers to Germany. We think there is a potential market for our products in Spain.

Sr González: **Ah, sí. Y ¿qué productos fabrican Vds.?**

You: Our factories in England make electronic typewriters. On the other hand, your company specializes in office equipment, doesn't it?

Sr González: **Eso es. Llevamos diez años exportando a otros países europeos.**

You: I see you are specialists in this field. This is what we are looking for.

FLUENCY PRACTICE 17

¿Cuánto tiempo?   ('How long?')

Using **llevar** + **present participle**, make up sentences with the words given, saying how long you or other people have been doing something.

Here is an example:

Yo/llevar/dos años/vivir en Londres
Yo llevo dos años viviendo en Londres
I've been living in London for 2 years

New word: **media hora**   half an hour

a) ellos/llevar/una hora/hablar con el director
b) vosotros/llevar/dos días/esperar la carta
c) yo/llevar/media hora/escribir el informe
d) tú/llevar/diez años/trabajar en Nueva York
e) él/llevar/seis años/vender equipos de oficina

Setting up business in Spain

> In this unit, you will learn more about verbs in the present tense, and how to use direct object pronouns.
>
> Mr Jackson and señorita Martín turn to practical problems of living and working in the big cities ...

Señorita Martín: ¿Cree Vd. que España puede ser un mercado potencial para su compañía?

Mr Jackson: Sí. Ya estamos establecidos en Francia donde gozamos de una reputación muy buena, y acabamos de abrir una oficina en Alemania. A pesar de la recesión mundial, la compañía está en un proceso de expansión y creemos que es el momento oportuno para considerar la posibilidad de establecernos aquí en Madrid.

Señorita Martín: ¿Y dónde están ubicadas sus sucursales extranjeras?

Mr Jackson: Nuestra oficina francesa se encuentra en las afueras de París. Desde el punto de vista logístico, tiene mayor ventaja estar allí que en pleno centro.

Señorita Martín: Sí, estoy de acuerdo.

Mr Jackson: Asimismo, nuestro representante en Alemania que actualmente tiene su sede en el centro bancario de Francfort, va a trasladarse a los alrededores al final de este año.

Señorita Martín: Nosotros tenemos nuestras oficinas principales en Alcobendas desde hace un par de años. Hoy día los alquileres en el centro son demasiado altos. El transporte público no es muy bueno y hay mucha gente que no quiere trabajar en el centro debido a los problemas de tráfico y contaminación, e incluso prefiere vivir en las afueras ya que es más fácil y en muchas ocasiones más económico.

Mr Jackson: Lo comprendo. Parece que la mayoría de las grandes ciudades padecen de las mismas dificultades.

Señorita Martín: Sí. ¡Tenemos muchos problemas en común! Sin embargo, nuestro mercado presenta unos aspectos muy específicos en comparación, por ejemplo, con Francia. ¿Qué circunstancias en particular conducen a su compañía a decidir probar el mercado aquí?

TRANSLATION

Señorita Martín: You think that Spain can be a potential market for your company?

Mr Jackson: Yes. We are already (lit. already we are) established in France where we have (lit. enjoy of) a very good reputation (lit. a reputation very good), and we have just opened (lit. we finish from opening) an office in Germany. Despite the world recession (lit. recession worldwide), the company is in a process of expansion and we believe that now is the right time (lit. it is the moment appropriate) to consider the possibility of setting up (ourselves) here in Madrid.

Señorita Martín: And where are your foreign branches located (lit. where are located your branches foreign)?

Mr Jackson: Our French office (lit. office French) is situated (lit. finds itself) on the outskirts of Paris. From the logistical point of view, it is more advantageous (lit. it has bigger advantage) to be there than right in the centre (lit. in complete centre).

Señorita Martín: Yes, I agree (lit. I am in agreement).

Mr Jackson: Similarly, our representative in Germany who at the moment has his head office in the financial quarter (lit. centre) of Frankfurt, is going to move to the outskirts at the end of this year.

Señorita Martín: We have had our main offices in Alcobendas for a couple of years now (lit. we have our offices main in Alcobendas since a couple of years ago). Today the rents in the centre are too high. The public transport is not good, there are many people who don't want to work in the centre because of the problems of traffic and pollution, and (they) even prefer to live on the outskirts since it's easier (*lit.* more easy) and in many instances cheaper (*lit.* more economical).

Mr Jackson: I understand that (*lit.* it I understand). It seems that the majority of the big cities suffer from the same difficulties.

Señorita Martín: Yes. We have many problems in common! However, our market has (*lit.* displays) some very specific aspects compared (*lit.* in comparison), for example, with France. What circumstances in particular lead your company to decide to try out the market here?

Checklist 4

Expressions:

a pesar de	in spite of, despite
el momento oportuno	the right time
debido a	because of, due to
en muchas ocasiones	in many instances, many times, often
en pleno centro	right in the centre
hay	there is, there are
en común	in common, mutual
sin embargo	however, nonetheless
en particular	in particular
desde hace	for (in expressions of time)

Proper Names:

París	Paris
Francfort	Frankfurt

Masculine nouns:

el proceso	the process
el punto de vista	the point of view
el centro	the centre
el par	the couple, pair
el transporte	the transport
el problema	the problem
el tráfico	the traffic
el aspecto	the aspect, side
el alquiler	the rent
el ejemplo	the example
los alrededores	the outskirts
el final	the end

Feminine nouns:

la reputación	the reputation
la recesión	the recession
la expansión	the expansion
la posibilidad	the possibility
la sucursal	the branch, branch office
las afueras	the outskirts
la gente	the people
la contaminación	the pollution, contamination
la ocasión	the occasion, time
la mayoría	the majority
la dificultad	the difficulty
la circunstancia	the circumstance

Adjectives:

potencial	potential
mundial	worldwide, universal, of the world
oportuno	opportune, appropriate
logístico	logistical
mayor	greater, bigger
pleno	full, complete
principal	main, principal
francés	French
alto	high
público	public
económico	economic(al)
más	more
mismo	same
ubicado	located, situated
específico	specific
establecido	established
bancario	financial, banking

Verbs:

acabar	to finish
acabar de ...	to have just ...
ir	to go
trasladarse	to move (to a place)
querer	to want, wish, love someone
preferir	to prefer
gozar de	to enjoy, have, possess
trabajar	to work
poder	to be able
considerar	to consider
establecerse	to set up, establish oneself
estar ubicado	to be situated

encontrarse	to be situated, to find oneself
estar de acuerdo	to be in agreement, to agree
comprender	to understand
parecer	to seem
padecer de	to suffer from
presentar	to present, show, display, have
probar	to test, sample, try (out)

Conjunctions:

que	than
e (y)	and (see Checknote 48)

Interrogative:

¿dónde?	where?

Relative adverb:

donde	where

Preposition:

desde	from

Adverbs:

hoy día	nowadays
incluso	even
demasiado	too
allí	there
actualmente	at the moment, at present, nowadays
asimismo	similarly, in the same way

CHECKNOTES

34 Stem-changing verbs:

Certain verbs change their 'stem' in parts of the present tense. Their endings do, however, follow the rules for regular verbs. To simplify matters, we can divide these verbs into three groups:

Group 1:

Verbs in this group change the 'e' to an 'ie':

Here are some examples:

a) -AR verbs like **empezar** ('to begin')

empi**e**zo	I begin
empi**e**zas	you begin (*fam. sing.*)
empi**e**za	he/she/it begins
	you begin (*pol. sing.*)
empezamos	we begin
empezáis	you begin (*fam. pl.*)
empi**e**zan	they begin
	you begin (*pol. pl.*)

Others like this are:

pensar	to think, intend
cerrar	to close
sentarse	to sit down (this verb is also reflexive. In fact you've already come across it in Unit 1!)

Example:

La reunión empieza a las tres.
The meeting starts at three o'clock.

b) -ER verbs like **querer** ('to want'). (This verb was first introduced in Unit 1.) Here's the whole present tense:

qui**e**ro	I want
qui**e**res	you want (*fam. sing.*)
qui**e**re	he/she/it wants
	you want (*pol. sing.*)
queremos	we want
queréis	you want (*fam. pl.*)
qui**e**ren	they want
	you want (*pol. pl.*)

Other verbs like this are:

entender   'to understand'
perder   'to lose'

Example:

> **Quiere vivir en Madrid.**
> She wants to live in Madrid.

c) **-IR** verbs like **invertir** ('to invest')

invierto	I invest
inviertes	you invest (*fam. sing.*)
invierte	he/she/it invests
	you invest (*pol. sing.*)
invertimos	we invest
invertís	you invest (*fam. pl.*)
invierten	they invest
	you invest (*pol. pl.*)

Others like this are:

preferir   'to prefer'
sentir   'to regret'
referirse   'to refer' (this is reflexive as well!)

Example:

> **Se refiere al informe.**   He refers to the report.

Group 2:

This group of stem-changing verbs changes the **o** to **ue**:

a) **-AR** verbs like **probar** ('to test')

pruebo	I test
pruebas	you test (*fam. sing.*)
prueba	he/she/it tests
	you test (*pol. sing.*)
probamos	we test
probáis	you test (*fam. pl.*)
prueban	they test
	you test (*pol. pl.*)

Others like this are:

encontrar   'to meet'

encontrarse   'to find oneself'
almorzar   'to have lunch'
mostrar   'to show'

Example:

Almuerzo a las dos.   I have lunch at two o'clock.

b) -**ER** verbs like **poder** ('to be able to') (this verb featured in Unit 1). Now here is the rest of the present tense:

puedo   I am able, can
puedes   you are able, can (*fam. sing.*)
puede   he/she/it is able, can
    you are able, can (*pol. sing.*)
podemos   we are able, can
podéis   you are able, can (*fam. pl.*)
pueden   they are able, can
    you are able, can (*pol. pl.*)

Others like this are:

volver   'to return, go back'

Example:

No puedo trabajar aquí.   I can't work here.

c) -**IR** verbs like **dormir** ('to sleep')

duermo   I sleep
duermes   you sleep (*fam. sing.*)
duerme   he/she/it sleeps
    you sleep (*pol. sing.*)
dormimos   we sleep
dormís   you sleep (*fam. pl.*)
duermen   they sleep
    you sleep (*pol. pl.*)

Another like this is:

morir   'to die'

Example:

Duerme bien.   He sleeps well.

Group 3:

Some -IR verbs change the **e** to an **i** in the stem of parts of the present tense. Here is an example:

pedir	'to ask for (something)'
pi̱do	I ask for
pi̱des	you ask for (*fam. sing.*)
pi̱de	he/she/it asks for
	you ask for (*pol. sing.*)
pedimos	we ask for
pedís	you ask for (*fam. pl.*)
pi̱den	they ask for
	you ask for (*pol. pl.*)

Others like this are:

decir	'to say' (you met this verb in Unit 3)
servir	'to serve'
repetir	'to repeat'

Example:

El director pide una cerveza.
The director asks for a beer.

35 **Acabar de** ('to have just' + **past participle**)

Acabar is a regular **-AR** verb and when used on its own means 'to finish':

Quiero acabar la reunión a las dos.
I want to finish the meeting at two o'clock.

But **acabar** used with **de** + **infinitive** is a very handy way of saying that someone has just done something or something has just happened. For example:

Acabo de recibir la carta.	I have just received the letter.
El presidente acaba de hablar.	The president has just spoken.
¿Acabáis de llegar?	Have you just arrived?

36 The verb **ir** ('to go')

This verb is irregular in the present tense. Since it isn't used in the present continuous tense, the present tense conveys the continuous meaning as well. Here is the full conjugation:

voy	I go, I am going
vas	you go, you are going
va	he/she/it goes, he/she/it is going
	you go, you are going
vamos	we go, we are going
vais	you go, you are going
van	they go, they are going
	you go, you are going

Here are examples of the verb in use:

Van a la oficina. They go to the office.

Este año vamos al sur de Francia.
This year we're going to the south of France.

It's worth noting that **vamos**, as well as meaning 'we go' or 'we are going', is used to denote 'let's go'. For example:

Vamos al bar. – Sí, vamos.
Let's go to the bar. – Yes, let's.

Vamos, María, ya son las ocho.
Let's go, Mary, it's already eight o'clock.

37 IR + a + infinitive

Ir combined with another verb is used to express a future intention. The second verb is always in the infinitive, but don't forget to add in the preposition **a**. For example:

Voy a trabajar en Madrid.
I am going to work in Madrid.

¿Van a asistir a la reunión?
Are they going to attend the meeting?

38 Two verbs together without a preposition

You've learnt that some verbs (like **acabar de** and **ir a**) require the preposition when used with another verb. However some don't and here are a few to learn. Remember the second verb is always in the infinitive in Spanish even though it isn't in the English:

a) **querer** ('to want')

Queremos salir.	We want to go out.
Quiere leer.	She wants to read.

b) **decidir** ('to decide')

Deciden volver.	They decide to go back/return.
Decide llamar.	She decides to call.

c) **deber** ('must')

Debo asistir.	I must attend.
Debemos responder.	We must reply.

d) **poder** ('can')

No podemos importar.	We cannot import.
¿Puedes volver a las cinco?	Can you come back at five?

e) **pensar** ('intend, thinking of')

Piensan especializarse.	They intend specializing.
Pienso ir a Madrid.	I'm thinking of going to Madrid.

39 Gozar de ('to enjoy', 'have', 'possess' (something good/advantageous))

Don't forget the preposition **de** when you use this verb. For example:

La compañía goza de una buena reputación.
The company has a good reputation.

Gozan de las ventajas.	They enjoy the advantages.

40 Padecer ('to suffer') establecer ('to establish') Parecer ('to seem')

These three verbs follow the same pattern as **conocer** in the present tense. (See Checknote 28.)

41 Conducir a ('to lead to')

Don't forget the preposition **a**. For example:

Estas circunstancias van a conducir a muchos problemas.
These circumstances are going to lead to many problems.

Las dificultades nos conducen a considerar otros mercados.
The difficulties lead us to consider other markets.

42 Hay

This useful little word means 'there is' and 'there are', for example:

Hay mucho tráfico.   There is a lot of traffic.

Hay diez empresas británicas que fabrican estas máquinas.
There are ten British companies which manufacture these machines.

43 Desde ('from')

Desde and **de** meaning 'from' are often interchangeable:

Me llama desde/de la oficina.
He calls me from the office.

Desde does, however, tend to be more emphatic than **de**, and is used freely in expressions of time:

Desde mi punto de vista.
From my point of view.

Desde ahora voy a hablar en español.
From now (on) I'm going to speak in Spanish.

Trabajo desde las ocho.
I work from 8 o'clock.

44 Comparison of adjectives

In English comparisons are made by adding **-er** to the adjective or by adding 'more/less'. In Spanish, we simply put **más** ('more') or **menos** ('less') before the adjective.

For example:

La fábrica es grande.	The factory is big.
La fábrica es más grande.	The factory is bigger.
Su oficina es muy moderna.	Their office is very modern.
Nuestra oficina es menos moderna.	Our office is less modern.

There are some exceptions:

mayor	greater, older
menor	smaller, lesser, younger
mejor	better
peor	worse

These adjectives often go before the noun. They also have no separate feminine form:

La contaminación es peor en el centro.
The pollution is worse in the centre.

Este bar es mejor.
This bar is better.

Hoy día los problemas son mayores.
Nowadays the problems are greater.

Esas máquinas son peores.
Those machines are worse.

We translate 'than' by using **que**:

Londres es más grande que Madrid.
London is bigger than Madrid.

La contaminación es peor en Madrid que en Barcelona.
The pollution is worse in Madrid than in Barcelona.

45 **La gente** ('(the) people')

In English this noun takes a plural verb. In Spanish, however, it is considered singular. For example:

La gente es española.
The people are (*lit.* is) Spanish.

Hay mucha gente que habla inglés.
There are many people who speak (*lit.* speaks) English.

46 Direct object pronouns

Study the following:

me	me
te	you (*fam. sing.*)
le	him, you (*pol. m. sing.*)
la	her, you (*pol. f. sing.*)
lo	it (*m.*)
la	it (*f.*)
nos	us
os	you (*fam. pl.*)
les	them (*m.*), you (*pol. m. pl.*)
las	them (*f.*), you (*pol. f. pl.*)
los	them (*m.*) referring to things
las	them (*f.*) referring to things

In Spain and Latin America, **lo** and **los** can also be used instead of **le** and **les**.

Like the reflexive pronouns, these pronouns usually go before the verb, NOT after, as in English. For example:

Te creo.	I believe you.
La escribe. (la carta)	She writes it. (the letter)
Nos espera.	He is expecting us.

When an infinitive is involved, the pronoun can be tagged on the end of it or placed before the verb phrase, but never in the middle. For example:

No puedo acompañarte.
No te puedo acompañar. } I can't accompany you.

Decide llamaros.
Os decide llamar. } She decides to call you.

The same applies when the present participle is used. For example: (Note the accent on the participle to maintain the original stress)

Está explicándolo.
Lo está explicando. } He is explaining it.

47 Desde hace ('for' in expressions of time)

In Unit 3 (see Checknote 30) you learnt how to use the verb **llevar** to express how long something has been and is still going on. An alternative way is by using ...

... <u>present</u> tense of verb + **desde hace** + time.

For example:

Vivo aquí desde hace doce años.
I have been living (and still am) here for twelve years.

Aprendemos español desde hace un año.
We've been learning Spanish for a year.

48 E ('and')

The Spanish for 'and', normally **y**, changes to **e** before a word beginning with an 'i' or an 'hi'. For example:

españoles e italianos
Spanish and Italian

una ciudad interesante e histórica
an interesting and historic city

49 Alcobendas

This is an area on the outskirts of Madrid where many companies have set up their offices and factories in recent years.

50 Relative pronoun que

This means both 'which' and 'who'. For example:

los aspectos que consideramos
the aspects which we are considering

el señor que quiere hablar
the man who wants to speak

Comprehension Practice 4

Before you answer these questions on the dialogue, study the new words which are used in the questions:

New words:

el país	the country	**alemán**	German
¿Cuándo?	when?	**¿Cómo?**	How?

1 ¿Qué país representa un nuevo mercado para Excel-Equip?
2 ¿Dónde acaba de abrir una oficina?
3 ¿Se encuentra su sucursal francesa en el centro de París?
4 ¿Cuándo va a trasladarse a las afueras de Francfort el representante alemán?
5 ¿Cómo son los alquileres en el centro de Madrid?
6 ¿Qué problemas tienen las grandes ciudades?

FLUENCY PRACTICE 18

Your Spanish counterpart asks you and a colleague to clarify various points. Reply on behalf of both yourself and the colleague, as in the example. Take the words in brackets as your cue.

Note that your counterpart is using the familiar 'you' form (**vosotros**) since you know each other reasonably well.

New word: **un/una colega**   a colleague

Example:

¿Queréis café? (un té)
Do you want coffee?/Would you like coffee?
Mi colega, sí, pero yo quiero un té.
My colleague, yes, but I want a tea.

a) ¿Volvéis a Inglaterra a las ocho? (**a las 10**)
b) ¿Preferís trabajar en Madrid? (**Barcelona**)
c) ¿Os referís al informe? (**la carta**)
d) ¿Podéis empezar a las nueve? (**a las 8**)
e) ¿Pensáis importar equipos de Alemania? (**Francia**)

FLUENCY PRACTICE 19

At a meeting, your Spanish client wishes to know more about your company. Answer his/her questions, using the words in brackets for your answers. Remember you are representing the company, so your answers will probably use the plural 'we' and the appropriate ending of the verb.

For example:

¿Dónde tienen Vds. fábricas? (in Spain and France)
Where do you have factories?
Tenemos fábricas en España y en Francia.
We have factories in Spain and France.

a) ¿Dónde quieren Vds. exportar ordenadores? (to Italy)
b) ¿Cuándo van Vds. a abrir una nueva oficina? (at the end of the year)
c) ¿Cuánto tiempo llevan Vds. exportando a Alemania? (a couple of years)
d) ¿En qué países invierten Vds.? (Germany and France)
e) ¿Dónde piensan Vds. establecerse en España? (in Málaga)
f) ¿A qué hora cierran Vds. la oficina? (at 7)

FLUENCY PRACTICE 20

One-upmanship is not an attitude you normally adopt, but perhaps business competitors need reminding from time to time of the superiority of your company and products. Imagine some conversations along these lines:

New word: pocos   few

> *Competitor:* **Nuestra compañía es muy grande.**
> Our company is very big.
>
> *You:* **¿Ah, sí? Mi compañía es más grande.**
> Really? My company is bigger.

a) Nuestras oficinas son muy modernas.
b) Nuestros productos son muy buenos.
c) Exportamos muchos ordenadores a España.
d) Nuestro personal trabaja mucho.
e) Nuestra empresa tiene pocos problemas.

FLUENCY PRACTICE 21

Take part in this short conversation with a Spanish colleague about opening up an office in Spain. Look back at the main dialogue of this unit and the Checknotes to remind yourself of some of the words and structures.

New words:

ayudar	to help
mañana	tomorrow

> *Colleague:* **Tengo entendido que Vds. van a abrir una sucursal en Valladolid.**
>
> *You:* Yes. Despite the difficulties, we think it is the right time to test the Spanish market.
>
> *Colleague:* **Sí, pero desde el punto de vista logístico, Madrid tiene mayor ventaja, ¿no?**
>
> *You:* Well ... the rents in Madrid are higher than in Valladolid. It's a smaller town, the public transport is good and it has less pollution. We think people prefer to work and live there.
>
> *Colleague:* **Sí, es verdad. Bueno, ¿podemos ayudarles a buscar unas oficinas?**
>
> *You:* Oh, thank you. Our director has just arrived today, and we are thinking of going to Valladolid tomorrow.

FLUENCY PRACTICE 22

Using the verb **acabar de** ('to have just'), make sentences using the following words:

Example:

Miss López/go out

La señorita López acaba de salir.
Miss López has just gone out.

a) The director/begin the meeting
b) We/read the report
c) Mr and Mrs González/get up
d) That man over there/return from New York
e) I/call you (*fam. sing.*)

FLUENCY PRACTICE 23

Answer these questions using the correct direct object pronoun. Watch the verb! If it is singular, then you will reply with 'I', if it is plural, then use 'we'.

Example:

¿Escribes las cartas?
Do you (singular) write the letters?

Sí, las escribo.
Yes, I write them. (*lit.* them I write).

¿Bebéis café?
Do you (plural) drink coffee?

Sí, lo bebemos.
Yes, we drink it.

a) ¿Lees el informe?
b) ¿Buscáis a Juan?
c) ¿Estás ayudando a María?
d) ¿Quieren Vds. explicar el problema?
e) ¿Prefiere Vd. té?

FLUENCY PRACTICE 24

New word: esperar   to wait for

Imagine you are burdened with endless responsibilities and have to refuse invitations and suggestions from colleagues. Use the cues in brackets for your answers.

Example:

> *Colleague:*   ¿Quieres tomar una cerveza en el bar?
> Do you want to have a beer in the bar?
>
> *You:*   (be in the office at 2)
> **No puedo. Debo estar en la oficina a las dos.**
> I can't. I must be in the office at two.

a) *Colleague:*   ¿Vamos a la reunión?
   You: (write a letter to the director)

b) *Colleague:*   ¿Vamos a comer con el señor López?
   You: (be present at a meeting in Alcobendas)

c) *Colleague:*   ¿Vas a volver al hotel ahora?
   You: (wait for Miss Martín)

d) *Colleague:*   Esperas a la señorita López, ¿verdad?
   You: (return to the hotel immediately)

e) *Colleague:*   ¿Quieres ayudarnos a abrir las cartas?
   You: (explain the main aspects of the report to the directors)

*Spain is divided into 17 **Comunidades Autónomas** (Autonomous Regions), each with its own special identity.*

EL MAPA DE ESPAÑA
[COMUNIDADES AUTÓNOMAS]

The Spanish television network also represents the regions, with special local channels.

AUTONÓMICAS

TELEMADRID

7.30 **Tráfico.**
8.30 **La banda.** Incluye:
— 8.30 *Los defensores de la Tierra.*
— 8.50 *Fuerza G, guardianes del espacio.*
— 9.15 *Los diminutos*
9.35 **Allo, allo.**
10.00 **Avance informativo.**
10.10 **Madrid directo.**
11.10 **La banda.** Espacio infantil que incluye:
— *Doraemon, el gato cósmico.*
— *Los dinosaurios.*

TVG

10.25 **Preescolar na casa.**
10.55 **Fauna.**
11.25 **A familia Mudanza.**
12.25 **Informativo especial para xordos.**
12.30 **Mar de fondo.**
12.35 **Mister Ed.**
13.00 **A cociñar.**
13.10 **Telenovela.** *Paraíso.*
14.00 **Telexornal comarcas.**
14.20 **A saúde.**
14.25 **Tempo e agro.**
14.30 **Telexornal 1.**

ETB-1

12.10 **Aurkezpena.**
12.10 **Duplex.**
12.40 **Iparraldearen orena.**
12.45 **Gaur egun Euskal Herria.**
13.00 **Gaur egun.** Informativo.
13.30 **Gadget inspektorea.**
13.55 **Barkleytarrak.**
14.15 **Dinky Diak.**
14.45 **Pluche riquet eta pat.**
15.10 **Sustraia.**
15.40 **Txuri beltz.**

Discussing markets

In this unit, we introduce you to a past tense – the perfect tense. The conversation between Mr Jackson and señorita Martín turns to the topic of markets.

Mr Jackson:	Señorita Martín, puedo asegurarla que tanto la compañía como nuestros productos tienen una excelente reputación y nuestros precios son muy competitivos.
Señorita Martín:	Sí, pero como ya le he comentado, hay que tener en cuenta que el mercado español es muy complicado.
Mr Jackson:	De acuerdo. Damos por hecho que existen diferencias entre España y otros países europeos. Hemos realizado un estudio de mercado, y los resultados han sido muy favorables.
Señorita Martín:	¿Y esto les ha hecho pensar que sus productos pueden tener éxito aquí?
Mr Jackson:	Exactamente. Creemos que en los últimos años España ha hecho frente a la competencia de otras naciones desarrolladas y seguramente su economía va a mantenerse en una línea favorable.
Señorita Martín:	¡Es Vd. muy optimista! Es verdad que España se ha desarrollado muy rápidamente en la última década pero mucha gente cree que no vamos a poder superar las dificultades actuales.
Mr Jackson:	En Gran Bretaña también estamos experimentando problemas económicos. El volumen de ventas de nuestro mercado ha disminuido bastante este año. Por eso nos dirigimos al mercado europeo con la intención de ampliar nuestra área de ventas, y así mejorar

nuestras tasas de crecimiento. Los mercados se hacen cada vez más internacionales y el Mercado Único nos da la oportunidad que hemos estado esperando.

Señorita Martín: Tiene razón al respecto. Se debe tener una mentalidad más abierta a nuevos mercados.

TRANSLATION

Mr Jackson: Señorita Martín, I can assure you that both (*lit.* as much) the company and (*lit.* as) our products have an excellent reputation and our prices are very competitive.

Señorita Martín: Yes, but as I was saying (*lit.* to you have commented), one has to bear in mind that the Spanish market is very complicated.

Mr Jackson: Yes, of course (*lit.* of agreement). We accept (*lit.* concede as fact) that differences exist (*lit.* exist differences) between Spain and other European countries. We have carried out a market study and the results have been very favourable.

Señorita Martín: And this has made you (*lit.* you has made) think that your products can be successful (*lit.* have success) here?

Mr Jackson: Exactly. We believe that in the last (few) years Spain has met (*lit.* faced) the competition from other developed nations and no doubt her economy will (*lit.* is going to) maintain (*lit.* keep itself on) a favourable course.

Señorita Martín: You are (*lit.* are you) very optimistic! It is true (*lit.* truth) that Spain has developed very quickly over (*lit.* in) the last decade but many people think that we are not going to be able to overcome the present difficulties.

Mr Jackson: In Great Britain, we too are (*lit.* also we are) experiencing economic problems. The turnover of (*lit.* volume of sales) our (home) market has decreased somewhat this year. For that (reason) we are turning (*lit.* we direct ourselves) to the European market with the intention of broadening our sales area and so improve our growth rates (*lit.* rates of growth). The markets are becoming more and more (*lit.* each time more) international and the Single Market gives us (*lit.*

us gives) the opportunity (which) we have been
waiting for.

Señorita Martín: You are right (*lit.* you have reason) in that (*lit.* to the)
respect. One must be more broadminded about (*lit.*
have a mentality more open to) new markets.

Checklist 5

Expressions:

hay que	one has to
de acuerdo	yes of course, agreed
por eso	and so, therefore
cada vez más	more and more, increasingly
al respecto	in that respect
tanto ... como ...	both ... (a) and ... (b)

Proper names:

Gran Bretaña	Great Britain

Masculine nouns:

el precio	the price
el estudio	the study, survey
el resultado	the result
el volumen	the volume
el volumen de ventas	the turnover, volume of sales
el crecimiento	the growth

Feminine nouns:

la venta	the sale
la diferencia	the difference
la competencia	the competition
la nación	the nation
la economía	the economy
la línea	the line, course
la década	the decade
el área	the area (see Checknote 56)
la tasa de crecimiento	the growth-rate
la mentalidad	the mentality, mental attitude

Verbs:

asegurar	to assure
comentar	to comment (on), mention
tener en cuenta	to bear in mind

dar por hecho	to accept/consider/take as fact
realizar	to carry out
hacer	to make, do
tener éxito	to be successful
hacer frente a	to face, confront, stand up to
mantenerse	to keep, maintain oneself
desarrollarse	to develop, evolve (oneself)
superar	to overcome
experimentar	to experience
dirigirse a	to go to, turn towards
ampliar	to enlarge, expand, widen, extend
mejorar	to improve
hacerse	to become
tener razón	to be right

Irregular verbs:

hacer 'to do, make'
Present: **hago, haces, hace, hacemos, hacéis, hacen**
Perfect: **he hecho**

dar 'to give, concede'
Present: **doy, das, da, damos, dais, dan**
Perfect: **he dado**

disminuir 'to diminish, decrease'
Present: **disminuyo, disminuyes, disminuye, disminuimos, disminuís, disminuyen**
Perfect: **he disminuido**

Adjectives:

actual	present
competitivo	competitive
excelente	excellent
complicado	complicated
favorable	favourable
último	last
desarrollado	developed
optimista	optimistic
internacional	international
abierto	open
nuevo	new

Conjunction:

como	as

Preposition:

entre	between, amongst

Adverbs:

exactamente	exactly
rápidamente	quickly
seguramente	for sure, surely
bastante	somewhat, fairly
así	so, in this way, thus

CHECKNOTES

51 The perfect tense

Examples of the perfect tense in English are 'I have worked', 'he/she has written', 'we have said', etc. In Spanish this tense is formed with the present tense of **haber** ('to have') followed by the past participle of the appropriate verb.

First here's how to form the past participle. Add **-ado** to the stem of **-AR** verbs, and **-ido** to the stem of **-ER** and **-IR** verbs, like this:

hablar → hablado ('spoken')
comer → comido ('eaten')
vivir → vivido ('lived')

And now here's the whole perfect tense:

haber trabajado	'to have worked'
he trabajado	I have worked
has trabajado	you have worked
ha trabajado	he/she/it has worked
	you have worked
hemos trabajado	we have worked
habéis trabajado	you have worked
han trabajado	they have worked
	you have worked

Haber is an 'auxiliary verb' used only in conjunction with other parts of the verb, in this case the past participle. So don't confuse it with **tener** 'to have, possess'. For example:

Tiene muchos problemas.	He has lots of problems.
Ha trabajado mucho hoy.	He has worked a lot today.

The perfect tense in Spanish is used in the same way as in English. For example:

Este año hemos vendido más.	This year we have sold more.

Like English, too, there are irregular past participles, though they are not always the same verbs! Here are a few:

hacer   → hecho ('done', 'made')
decir   → dicho ('said')
escribir → escrito ('written')
abrir   → abierto ('opened')
volver → vuelto ('returned')

However, unlike English, you can't separate the auxiliary from the past participle. Look at these examples:

Ya ha abierto la carta.
She has already opened the letter.

No hemos superado los problemas.
We have not overcome the problems.

¿Dónde ha estado Juan?
Where has John been?

If we combine the perfect tense of **estar** with the present participle (see Checknote 23), we can add a more continuous notion to the tense. For example:

he estado trabajando   I have been working
hemos estado buscando   we have been looking for

ha estado esperando esta oportunidad
he has been waiting for this opportunity

52 Idiomatic use of **tener** ('to have')

There are a number of idioms which use **tener** + **noun** where the English would use 'to be' + adjective. Here are some examples. (You've already met the first two in the dialogue):

tener éxito   to be successful (*lit.* to have success)
tener razón   to be right (*lit.* to have reason)
tener cuidado   to be careful (*lit.* to have care)
tener hambre   to be hungry
tener sed   to be thirsty

Tengo sed, voy a tomar una cerveza.
I'm thirsty, I'm going to have a beer.

La compañía ha tenido mucho éxito.
The company has been very successful (*lit.* has had much success).

53 Tanto ... como ... ('both ... and ...')

This means literally 'as much ... as ...' and is used when two things are considered equally:

tanto la secretaria como la recepcionista
both the secretary and the receptionist

debemos tener en cuenta tanto las ventajas como los problemas
we must bear in mind both the advantages and the problems

54 Hay que ('one has to, must')

In the last unit (Checknote 42) you learnt that **hay** means 'there is/are'. However when **que** is added, this little phrase, followed by the infinitive of a verb, is used to say, in an impersonal way, what must be done. Example:

Hay que buscar mercados nuevos.
One must look for new markets.

Hay que reservar el hotel.
You (in general) must book the hotel.

Remember that if a particular person is being referred to, you would be more likely to use **deber** (see Unit 3 and Checknote 38 in Unit 4):

Debe asistir a la reunión.	He must attend the meeting.
Hay que asistir a la reunión.	One must attend the meeting.

55 Adverbs

Lots of adverbs are formed in Spanish by adding the ending **-mente** to the <u>feminine</u> form of the adjective:

exacto	**exacta**	**exactamente**	exactly
rápido	**rápida**	**rápidamente**	quickly

When there is no specific feminine form, just take the adjective and add **-mente**:

fácil	**fácilmente**	easily
simple	**simplemente**	simply

56 El área ('the area')

If a feminine noun begins with stressed 'a' or 'ha' the masculine articles are used, but the noun remains feminine! Remember, however, that any accompanying adjective will have to be feminine!

Other nouns like this are:

el hambre   the hunger
un alza   a rise

Examples:

el área nueva   the new area
tengo mucha hambre   I'm very hungry (*lit.* I have much hunger)

57 a) Cada vez más ('more and more')

Instead of saying **más y más**, Spanish uses **cada vez más**. For example:

cada vez más gente piensa ...
more and more people think ...

unos problemas cada vez más complicados
more and more complicated problems

b) Cada vez menos ('less and less'/'fewer and fewer')

Similarly this structure avoids the clumsy **menos y menos**:

tenemos cada vez menos oportunidades
we have fewer and fewer opportunities

una situación cada vez menos favorable
an increasingly unfavourable situation

Comprehension Practice 5

Study these new words and then answer the questions on the dialogue.

el tipo	the sort, type
según	according to
la importancia	the importance

1 ¿Qué tipo de reputación tiene la compañía Excel-Equip?
2 ¿Cómo son los precios de la compañía?
3 Según la señorita Martín, ¿cómo es el mercado español?
4 ¿Qué es lo que dan por hecho el señor Jackson y su compañía?
5 ¿Qué ha hecho España en los últimos años?
6 ¿Cómo se ha desarrollado España en los últimos diez años?
7 ¿Están teniendo problemas los ingleses?
8 ¿A qué se dirige Excel-Equip?
9 ¿Qué quiere mejorar?
10 ¿Qué importancia tiene el Mercado Único para Excel-Equip?

FLUENCY PRACTICE 25

Imagine an office colleague asks if you are going to do something. You've anticipated the question and are able to say you've already done the task. You'll need to use the Perfect Tense and a direct object pronoun (see Checknote 46). Here's an example:

¿Vas a probar nuevos mercados?
Are you going to test new markets?

Ya los he probado.
I've already tested them.

New word: **convocar** to call, summon

a) ¿Vas a escribir las cartas?
b) ¿Va Vd. a realizar un estudio?
c) ¿No vas a terminar la cerveza?
d) ¿Vas a convocar una reunión?
e) ¿Va Vd. a abrir unas nuevas oficinas?

FLUENCY PRACTICE 26

You and a business associate seem to have many experiences in common. Following the example, make up sentences to explain that you too are experiencing or doing things along the same lines as your associate:

Associate: **Nuestra empresa se ha desarrollado mucho.**
Our company has developed a lot.

You: **Nosotros también estamos desarrollándonos mucho.**
We too are developing a lot.

a) La empresa se ha especializado en equipos electrónicos.
b) Mi compañía se ha dirigido al mercado español.
c) Nuestras sucursales se han hecho muy competitivas.
d) Nuestra empresa se ha trasladado a las afueras.
e) La empresa se ha mantenido en una línea favorable.

FLUENCY PRACTICE 27

New word: solucionar   to solve, resolve

Your day has been very busy, but you check through your diary with your secretary to see whether you have done everything. You'll need to use the perfect tense.

Example:

√ escribir/la carta/al Sr González
He escrito la carta al señor González,
(I've written the letter to Mr González,)

× hablar/con el director
pero, no he hablado con el director.
(but, I haven't spoken to the director.)

a) √ abrir/la oficina/a las 8
   × llamar a Ecofisa en Alcobendas
b) √ explicar/las dificultades/a la Srta Martín.
   × escribir/el informe
c) √ asistir a/la reunión a la 1
   × convocar/otra reunión/con los representantes
d) √ comer/con Juan/en el bar
   × solucionar/los problemas/con la recepcionista
e) √ empezar/el estudio de mercado
   × terminar/el informe económico

FLUENCY PRACTICE 28

Imagine a conversation with a Spanish agent during which you discuss markets and competitiveness:

Agent: **Hay que tener en cuenta que el mercado es muy complicado.**

You: As I was saying, the results of our market study make us think that our products can be successful in Spain.

Agent: **Sí, pero mucha gente cree que la economía no va a mantenerse en una línea favorable.**

You: Well, I am very optimistic, and I believe that the Single Market has given us an excellent opportunity to widen our sales area.

Agent: **Tiene razón al respecto. Por otra parte, hay que tener en cuenta que existe mucha competencia.**

You: Yes, one must always be careful in a very competitive market, but we can assure you that both our company and our machines have a good reputation.

FLUENCY PRACTICE 29

New words:

automatizado	automated
Holanda	Holland
Bélgica	Belgium

Answer these questions following the pattern of the example:

¿Importan Vds. equipos de Italia? (+ France)
Do you import equipment from Italy? (+ France)

Importamos equipos tanto de Italia como de Francia.
We import equipment both from Italy and (from) France.

a) ¿Fabrican Vds. máquinas electrónicas? (+ automated)
b) ¿Exportan Vds. equipos a Holanda? (+ Belgium)
c) ¿Tienen en cuenta los problemas? (+ advantages)
d) ¿Han considerado la posibilidad de establecer una oficina en el centro? (+ the outskirts)
e) ¿Se refieren Vds. al estudio de mercado? (+ economic report)

FLUENCY PRACTICE 30

New words:

difícil	difficult
aumentarse	to rise, go up, increase
mejorarse	to get better

Reviewing the last few years, you've noticed changes in the market and company performance. Following the examples, make up sentences using the words provided:

el mercado/hacerse/complicado

El mercado se ha hecho <u>cada vez más</u> complicado.
The market has become <u>more and more</u> complicated.

a) los problemas/hacerse/difíciles
b) los resultados/ser/favorables
c) nuestras tasas de crecimiento/mejorarse/rápidamente
d) el Mercado Único/dar/oportunidades
e) nuestras ventas/aumentarse/rápidamente

The picture isn't all positive! Follow the next example:

nuestros productos/tener/éxito en Francia

Nuestros productos han tenido cada vez menos éxito en Francia.
Our products have been <u>less and less</u> successful in France.

f) la economía/mantenerse/en una línea favorable
g) los precios/hacerse/competitivos
h) los alquileres/hacerse/económicos
i) la compañía/desarrollarse/rápidamente
j) nuestra compañía/exportar/máquinas a Europa

Reaching agreement

This unit introduces you to the future tense. Mr Jackson and señorita Martín go on to talk about the future collaboration between their two companies. Discussion leads to formal agreement, and so you will also learn how to write a letter in Spanish.

Mr Jackson:	Veo que compartimos la misma opinión. Si atravesamos las fronteras podremos aprovechar las oportunidades de la libre circulación de bienes. Sin embargo, hasta ahora no se han producido muchos cambios a este respecto en el mercado de la ofimática.
Señorita Martín:	Es verdad, muchas empresas han tardado en modernizar sus sistemas, y las que se han puesto al día, han tendido a comprar productos japoneses o americanos.
Mr Jackson:	Nuestra casa matriz es americana, está situada en Nueva York y como nuestro programa de expansión está financiado en parte por los americanos, creo que Vds. se darán cuenta de que la tecnología de los equipos es de vanguardia, que sus diseños son atractivos y modernos y que la calidad de su funcionamiento no tiene par.
Señorita Martín:	Desafortunadamente muchos de nuestros clientes son muy conservadores y será difícil tratar de cambiar unas ideas tan inflexibles, especialmente en lo que se refiere al equipo informático.
Mr Jackson:	Siempre hemos tenido en cuenta la necesidad de hacer compatibles nuestros productos con otros sistemas. Creo que hasta al cliente más conservador le interesarán los equipos de oficina que producimos.

Señorita Martín: En cuanto a la producción, España ya no es el país económico de antes; esperamos tasas de inflación muy elevadas en los próximos años.

Mr Jackson: De todos modos, pensamos que los costes son inferiores o equivalentes a los de Gran Bretaña.

Señorita Martín: Tienen una visión muy positiva del futuro mercado en este campo, y claro, si queremos mantener la competitividad, tendremos que buscar nuevas fuentes de suministro. Por eso, creo que estaremos dispuestos a incorporar equipos británicos a nuestra gama de productos, haciendo las modificaciones técnicas necesarias.

Mr Jackson: Perfecto. Ahora, ¿me permite enseñarle nuestros folletos? Luego podremos hablar de condiciones de entrega y de la forma de pago.

TRANSLATION

Mr Jackson: I see that we share the same opinion. If we cross the frontiers we will be able to take advantage of the opportunities of the free circulation/movement of goods. However, up till now, not many changes have come about (*lit.* not have been produced many changes) as regards this in the office automation market.

Señorita Martín: It's true, many companies have taken time to modernize their systems and the ones which have become (*lit.* put themselves) up to date have tended to buy Japanese or American products.

Mr Jackson: Our parent company is American (and) is situated in New York and since our expansion programme is financed in part by the Americans, I think that you will realize that the technology of the equipment is state of the art, that its designs are pleasing and modern and that the quality of (*lit.* its) performance is unique (*lit.* has no parallel).

Señorita Martín: Unfortunately many of our customers are very conservative and it will be difficult to try to change such inflexible ideas (*lit.* some ideas so inflexible), especially with regard to computer equipment.

Mr Jackson:	We have always (*lit.* always we have) borne in mind the need to make our products compatible (*lit.* make compatible our products) with other systems. I think that even the most conservative customer will be interested in (*lit.* even the customer most conservative him will interest) the office equipment which we produce.
Señorita Martín:	As regards production, Spain is no longer the cheap (*lit.* economical) country it used to be (*lit.* of before); we are expecting very high inflation rates in the next (few) years.
Mr Jackson:	At any rate, we believe that the costs are lower or the same as those (*lit.* the ones) in (*lit.* of) Great Britain.
Señorita Martín:	You have a very positive view of the future market in this field and, of course, if we want to maintain competitiveness, we will have to look for new sources of supply. For that reason, I think that we will be willing to incorporate British equipment into our range of products, making the necessary technical modifications.
Mr Jackson:	Perfect. Now, allow me (*lit.* me do you allow) to show you our brochures? Then we can (*lit.* will be able to) talk about terms of delivery and form of payment.

Checklist 6

Masculine nouns:

el bien	good (*gen.*)
los bienes	goods (*comm.*)
el cambio	change
el sistema	system
el programa	programme
el diseño	design
el funcionamiento	performance
el par	like, equal, par
el material	equipment, plant, materials
el coste	cost
el suministro	supply
el folleto	brochure, pamphlet
el pago	payment

Feminine nouns:

la opinión	opinion

la frontera	frontier
la circulación	circulation, movement
la casa matriz	parent company
la calidad	quality
la necesidad	need
la idea	idea
la producción	production
la inflación	inflation
la visión	view, vision
la competitividad	competitiveness
la fuente	source
la gama	range
la modificación	modification
la condición	condition, term
la entrega	delivery
la forma	form

Verbs:

compartir	to share
atravesar	to cross (stem-changing e → ie)
aprovechar	to take advantage of
producir	to produce, make (produzco, produces, etc)
producirse	to come about, arise
tardar en ...	to take (a long) time to ...
modernizar	to modernize
ponerse al día	to become/get up-to-date
darse cuenta de ...	to realize
tender a ...	to tend to ... (stem-changing e → ie)
tratar de ...	to try to ...
cambiar	to change
interesar	to interest
mantener	to keep, maintain (like tener)
tener que ...	to have to ...
incorporar	to incorporate, include
enseñar	to show, teach

Adjectives:

libre	free
japonés	Japanese
financiado	financed
de vanguardia	state of the art
atractivo	attractive
conservador	conservative
inflexible	inflexible
informático	of computers
compatible	compatible

elevado	high
próximo	next
inferior	lower
equivalente	equivalent
positivo	positive
futuro	future
dispuesto a	ready to, willing to
técnico	technical
necesario	necessary
perfecto	perfect

Adverbs:

ahora	now
desafortunadamente	unfortunately
tan	so
especialmente	especially
siempre	always
hasta	even
antes	before, formerly
luego	then

Prepositions:

hasta	up to, until
por	by

Expressions:

a este respecto	as regards this
en parte	in part
en lo que se refiere a	as regards
en cuanto a	as regards
de todos modos	at any rate, anyway
claro	of course, naturally
¿me permite . . .?	(Will you) allow me . . ./May I . . .?

Conjunctions:

si	if
o	or

Indirect object pronoun:

le	to you (*pol.*)

Demonstrative pronouns:

las que (*f.*)	those which
los de (*m.*)	those of

Irregular verbs:

ver 'to see'
Present: **veo, ves, ve, vemos, veis, ven**
Perfect: **he visto**

poner 'to put'
Present: **pongo, pones, pone, ponemos, ponéis, ponen**
Perfect: **he puesto**

CHECKNOTES

58 The future tense

This tense is formed by adding endings to the infinitive of the verb. For example:

ver	'to see'
ver<u>é</u>	I will see
ver<u>ás</u>	you will see
ver<u>á</u>	he/she/it will see/you will see
ver<u>emos</u>	we will see
ver<u>éis</u>	you will see
ver<u>án</u>	they will see
	you will see

There is only one set of endings for all the verbs:

Hablaré con el señor Jackson.
I'll speak with Mr Jackson.

Viviremos en Santander.
We will live in Santander.

Será muy fácil.
It'll be very easy.

Of course, there are some exceptions! Although the endings always follow the rule, some verbs have a different stem:

tener	→ **tendré**	('I will have')
poder	→ **podré**	('I will be able')
hacer	→ **haré**	('I will do, make')
decir	→ **diré**	('I will say, tell')
poner	→ **pondré**	('I will put')

Lo haremos enseguida.
We'll do it at once.

No podré asistir.
I won't be able to be present.

Se hará cada vez más difícil.
It'll become more and more difficult.

Of course, compounds of these verbs will also be irregular. For example:

Mantendremos nuestra presencia en el mercado.
We will maintain our presence in the market.

59 Masculine nouns ending in -a

Some words which end in **-a** (of Greek origin) are masculine. You've met **el problema, el sistema** and **el programa** already. Here are some others:

el tema	theme, subject, topic
el idioma	language
el mapa	map
el telegrama	telegram
el clima	climate

60 Si ('if')

Si usually introduces conditions, like these:

Si vuelvo a las dos, te llamaré.
If I get back at two, I'll call you.

Si los resultados son favorables, podemos considerar otros mercados.
If the results are favourable, we can consider other markets.

Don't confuse **si** ('if') with **sí** ('yes') which carries an accent!

61 Superlatives

You've already seen how to form and use comparative adjectives. To form the superlative, just include the appropriate article before the comparative adjective. Example:

Este mercado es el más complicado.
This market is the most complicated.

Nuestra empresa es la mejor.
Our company is the best.

When the adjective qualifies a noun preceded by 'the', or a possessive adjective, the adjective loses its article. For example:

su momento más importante
her most important moment

la ciudad más grande
the biggest city

After a superlative, 'in' is usually translated by **de**, like this:

la compañía más competitiva de Inglaterra
the most competitive company in England

los mejores productos del mercado
the best products on/in the market

62 Indirect object pronouns:

me	to me
te	to you
le	to him, to her, to it, to you (*pol.*)
nos	to us
os	to you
les	to them, to you (*pol.*)

Like the direct object pronouns (see Checknote 46), these pronouns precede the verb. For example:

Le doy la carta.
I give him the letter.

Me enseña el informe.
He shows me the report.

When two object pronouns come together, the indirect object pronoun is always placed first, like this:

Os los da.
He gives them to you.

Te lo leeremos.
We will read it to you.

In the case of two third person object pronouns coming together, something a little unexpected happens; in order to avoid the unpleasant sound resulting from two consecutive monosyllables beginning with 'l', the first object pronoun (either **le** or **les**) is changed to **se**, like this:

Se lo enseñamos.
We show it to him (or to her, them, you).

However, here's a way of avoiding any ambiguity:

Se lo doy a él.	I give it to him.
Se lo doy a ella.	I give it to her.
Se lo hemos enseñado a Vd.	We have shown it to you.
Se lo daré a Vds.	I'll give it to you.

63 Tan ('so')

Tan is used before an adjective or an adverb, like this:

El mercado es tan complicado que ...
The market is so complicated that ...

Lo hacen tan rápidamente que ...
They do it so quickly that ...

Note, however, that in phrases where the **tan + adjective** follows the noun, the English translation is slightly different. For example:

un mercado tan complicado
such a complicated market

64 Tanto/a ('so much')   Tantos/as ('so many')

These are adjectives which precede the noun.

Hay tanta competencia hoy día.
There is so much competition nowadays.

Tiene tantos problemas.
He has so many problems.

tanto can also be an adverb, for example:

Habla tanto.
She talks so much.

65 El que ('he/the one who', 'that/the one which')
La que ('she/the one who', 'that/the one which')
Los/las que ('those/the ones who/which')

El sistema que buscamos tiene que ser muy flexible; el que tienen Vds. es bastante tradicional.
The system we are looking for has to be very flexible; the one you have is fairly traditional.

Los que piensan así representan a la mayoría.
Those who think in this way represent the majority.

Las máquinas que fabricamos son electrónicas; las que fabrican Vds. son menos modernas.
The machines which we manufacture are electronic; the ones/those which you manufacture are less modern.

Similarly, using **de** ('of') instead of **que**, you can make sentences like these:

Nuestros diseños son nuevos; los de Ecofisa son tradicionales.
Our designs are new; those of Ecofisa are traditional.

Su idea es buena, pero la de Juan es mejor.
Her idea is good but John's (*lit.* the one of John) is better.

Comprehension Practice 6

Answer these questions on the dialogue.

1 ¿Qué comparten el señor Jackson y la señorita Martín?
2 ¿Dónde no se han producido muchos cambios?
3 ¿Qué han tendido a hacer las empresas modernas?
4 ¿Qué están financiando los americanos?
5 ¿Cómo son muchos de los clientes de Ecofisa?
6 ¿Qué esperan los españoles en los próximos años?
7 Según el señor Jackson, ¿cómo son los costes en España?
8 Para mantener la competitividad, ¿qué tendrá que hacer Ecofisa?
9 ¿Qué estará dispuesta a hacer la señorita Martín?
10 ¿Qué va a enseñar a la señorita Martín el señor Jackson?

FLUENCY PRACTICE 31

New words:

el trabajo	work, job
el tipo de interés	interest rate

Answer the following questions using the future tense, as in the example:

¿Has escrito la carta? — **No, la escribiré mañana.**
Have you written the letter? — No, I'll write it tomorrow.

1 ¿Has terminado el informe?
2 ¿Has hecho el trabajo?
3 ¿Han podido Vds. asistir hoy?
4 ¿Ha abierto Vd. la nueva oficina?
5 ¿Has cambiado la hora de la reunión?
6 ¿Habéis visto la nueva fábrica?
7 ¿Ha tenido María la entrevista?

8 ¿Se ha mejorado la situación?
9 ¿Ha bajado el tipo de interés?
10 ¿Han solucionado el problema los directores?

FLUENCY PRACTICE 32

New words:

peor	worse
el libro	book
probar	to taste (stem-changing o → ue)

Answer the following questions, as in the example:

¿Cómo es la fábrica?   (modern, seen)
What's the factory like?

Es la más moderna que hemos visto.
It's the most modern we have seen.

1 ¿Cómo es el tráfico de Madrid? (worst, experienced)
2 ¿Cómo es la comida? (best, tasted)
3 ¿Cómo son los resultados? (favourable, had)
4 ¿Cómo son los productos? (advanced, sold)
5 ¿Cómo es el trabajo? (difficult, done)

FLUENCY PRACTICE 33

New words:

la cuenta	bill
el camarero	waiter

Answer the following questions.

Example:

¿Vas a dar el libro a Juan?
Are you going to give the book to John?

Ya se lo he dado.
I've already given him it.

1 ¿Vas a enseñar el informe al director?
2 ¿Va Vd. a explicar la dificultad al cliente?
3 ¿Vas a pedir la cuenta al camarero?
4 ¿Vais a darnos los detalles?
5 ¿Vas a leerme la carta?

FLUENCY PRACTICE 34

Translate the following sentences into Spanish:

1 The results have not been so favourable this year.
2 He is so optimistic!
3 Will we be able to solve such a complicated problem?
4 There's such a lot of traffic in the city these days.
5 The costs are increasing so quickly.
6 We have experienced so many difficulties.

FLUENCY PRACTICE 35

New words:

utilizar	to use
Estados Unidos	USA

Make up sentences using the cues given, as shown in the example:

Las máquinas que fabricamos son tradicionales. (modern)
The machines which we manufacture are traditional.

Las que fabrican Vds. son modernas.
The ones which you manufacture are modern.

1 Los ordenadores que importamos son británicos. (German)
2 El sistema que utilizamos es muy tradicional. (more flexible)
3 Las fábricas que tenemos están situadas en las afueras. (centre)
4 Los diseños que buscamos tienen que ser de buena calidad. (modern and attractive)
5 Los productos que compramos se han desarrollado en Francia. (USA)

FLUENCY PRACTICE 36

New word: penetrar en   to penetrate, go into

Change the words in brackets to the correct part of the Spanish verb, in the present tense. Remember the preposition where necessary!

1 Los clientes (tend to) comprar equipos franceses.
2 Los franceses (try to) penetrar en el mercado.
3 Las compañías (must) buscar nuevas fuentes de suministro.
4 Nuestros competidores (take some time to) introducir sistemas flexibles.
5 Los costes (are going to) ser inferiores.

DICTIONARY PRACTICE 1

Back in London, Mr Jackson in reply to señorita Martín's accept-
ance to represent Excel-Equip in Spain, writes to confirm the terms
they have agreed. However, so that his fellow directors will know
what is going on, he'll need to summarize the main points of the
letter in English. With the help of the additional checklist, do this
summary of the letter for him. You may wish to use a dictionary as
well; Hugo's pocket Spanish dictionary will be perfectly adequate
for this purpose. Check afterwards with the Key.

EXCEL-EQUIP
LIMITED

400 Regent Street
London W1R 6XZ
Telephone: 071 654 3210 Telex: 1234 Fax: 071 765 4321

A division of the Excel-Equip Corporation, New York

Ref: PJ/mmp.
Señorita Mercedes Martín
Directora de Ventas
Ecofisa,
Apartado 39
29001 ALCOBENDAS
MADRID, Spain.   21 de abril de 199–

Estimada señorita Martín:

Agradecemos su carta del 16 del mes en curso en la que acepta
representar a nuestra empresa y comercializar nuestros productos en
España. Por la presente me complace confirmar los principales puntos de
nuestras conversaciones.

Les concederemos una comisión del 25 por ciento sobre todas las ventas, y
en este porcentaje se incluirán todos los gastos publicitarios y la
participación en ferias comerciales españolas. Deseamos recibir noticias de
la posible campaña publicitaria.

La entrega de los bienes se efectuará por camión directamente a sus
almacenes en Alcobendas, libre de gastos, en un plazo de tres a cuatro
semanas después del recibo del pedido. El pago de las facturas se realizará
a través de transferencia bancaria a nuestro banco (NatWest, Regent Street,
London W1) cada dos meses, con el importe de su comisión ya descontado.
Quisiéramos recibir un informe de ventas mensual.

Puesto que Vds. se encargarán del servicio postventa, pondremos
inmediatamente a su disposición un técnico bilingüe que podrá organizar
un curso de instrucción en su compañía.

Estamos seguros de que la colaboración entre nuestras compañías será
muy fructífera.

Un cordial saludo de

Peter Jackson

GERENTE DE VENTAS

Additional Checklist

Masculine nouns:

(el) abril	April
el apartado	PO Box
el punto	point
el porcentaje	percentage
el gasto	expense
el camión	lorry, truck
el almacén	store, warehouse
el plazo	period, term
el recibo	receipt
el pedido	order
el banco	bank
el mes	month
el importe	amount, cost
el servicio	service
el técnico	technician
el curso	course
el saludo	greeting

Feminine nouns:

la conversación	conversation, discussion
la comisión	commission
la participación	participation
la feria	fair
las noticias	news
la campaña	campaign
la semana	week
la factura	invoice
la transferencia	transfer
la disposición	disposal
la instrucción	training, instruction
la colaboración	collaboration

Adjectives:

estimado	dear, respected
publicitario	advertising
descontado	deducted
mensual	monthly
postventa	after-sales
bilingüe	bilingual
seguro	sure
fructífero	productive, fruitful, successful
cordial	cordial

Adverbs:

directamente	directly
inmediatamente	immediately

Prepositions:

sobre	on
después de	after
a través de	by (means of)
entre	between

Conjunction:

puesto que	since, as

Expressions:

en curso	current, present
por la presente	hereby, in this letter
el 25 por ciento	25 per cent
quisiéramos	we would like

Verbs:

agradecer	to thank (agradezco)
aceptar	to accept, agree to
comercializar	to market, trade
complacer	to please (complazco)
confirmar	to confirm
conceder	to grant, concede
incluir	to include (incluyo)
desear	to want, wish
efectuar	to make, bring about, effect
encargarse de	to be in charge of, be responsible for

FLUENCY PRACTICE 37

This exercise is also based on Mr Jackson's letter. <u>From memory</u>, supply the Spanish for:

1 Thank you for your letter.
2 I have pleasure in confirming . . .
3 All expenses will be included.
4 Delivery of the goods.
5 Payment of invoices will be made by bank transfer.
6 We would like to receive a monthly sales report.
7 You will be responsible for the after-sales service.
8 We will put at your disposal . . .
9 A technician will be able to arrange a training course.
10 We are sure the collaboration between our companies will be successful.

FLUENCY PRACTICE 38

New words:

adjuntar	to enclose
el catálogo	catalogue
la lista	list
rogar	to request (stem-changing o → ue)
el detalle	detail
saludar	to greet
enviar	to send
inmediato	immediate
atentamente	yours faithfully

Irregular verb:

saber 'to know (a fact)' or 'know (how to . . .)'
Present: **sé, sabes, sabe, sabemos, sabéis, saben**

Study this letter and then answer the questions below:

JUAN GONZÁLEZ S.A.
AVENIDA PRINCIPAL 44
35007 PALENCIA

EQUIPOS LÓPEZ S.A.
CALLE TORO 34
45021 VALLADOLID   30 de abril de 199–

Muy señores míos:

Acabo de recibir su carta fechada el 11 de abril en la que adjuntan su último catálogo y lista de precios.

Me interesan especialmente los equipos electrónicos, y les ruego enviarme más detalles sobre las máquinas de escribir.

Quisiera saber si podré realizar el pago a través de transferencia bancaria y si Vds. pueden efectuar entregas inmediatas.

Les saluda atentamente,

Javier González
DIRECTOR

Now answer these questions. Check with the Key.

1 When did Javier González receive the letter?
2 What was enclosed with the letter?
3 What is he most interested in?
4 What does he ask them to send him?
5 He has two queries – what are they?

FLUENCY PRACTICE 39

Imagine that you wish to write to thank a company for sending you information which you requested. You now wish to make further enquiries. Earlier in the day, you jotted down some notes in no particular order, as a guide to the letter. Here are the notes. Can you now construct your letter in Spanish?

a) su carta fechada el 12 de abril
b) un folleto informativo
c) Quisiera saber
d) Les saluda atentamente.
e) y les ruego enviarme
f) Acabo de recibir
g) Muy señores míos:
h) un servicio postventa
i) y si pueden efectuar
j) más detalles sobre
k) los contestadores automáticos
l) en la que adjunta
m) entregas inmediatas.
n) de sus productos.
o) el contestador 'Elegante'.
p) Me interesan especialmente
q) si Vds. ofrecen

Telephone conversation

This unit will introduce you to phrases and sentences involving the subjunctive together with some more practice in using the future tense. You'll learn also some important expressions for use on the telephone.

By now, Mr Jackson and señorita Martín have had many conversations and have moved over to using first names and the familiar forms of 'you' when addressing each other.

There have been some problems with the office equipment delivered to Ecofisa, and señorita Martín decides to telephone Mr Jackson in London. However, it's after 5.30 p.m. and the Excel-Equip offices have just closed so señorita Martín has to leave a message on the answering machine.

Señorita Martín: Buenas tardes. Soy Mercedes Martín de la empresa Ecofisa. Quisiera dejar un recado para Peter Jackson. Hemos recibido los materiales. Gracias por haberlos enviado tan rápidamente. Desgraciadamente parece que ha habido un pequeño problema con el embalaje. ¿Puede llamarme a la oficina mañana, miércoles, por la mañana, entre las ocho y las doce si le es posible? Muchas gracias.

Wednesday, 10.30 a.m. Mr Jackson rings Ecofisa.

Switchboard: Ecofisa, dígame.

Mr Jackson: Buenos días. Quisiera hablar con la señorita Martín, por favor.

Switchboard: ¿De parte de quién?

Mr Jackson: De Peter Jackson de la compañía Excel-Equip.

Switchboard: Perdone. No le oigo bien. ¿Puede repetir su nombre por favor?

Mr Jackson: Jackson, J-A-C-K-S-O-N.

Switchboard: Espere un momento ... ¿señor Jackson? ... ahora le paso con la señorita Martín.

Señorita Martín: Buenos días, Peter, gracias por llamarme tan pronto.

Mr Jackson: De nada, es lo mínimo que puedo hacer. Siento que hayas tenido algunos problemas con los equipos que os hemos mandado. ¿Qué ha ocurrido exactamente?

Señorita Martín: Bueno, no creo que sean problemas insuperables, pero es preferible solucionarlos cuanto antes, al menos antes del próximo envío. Al fin y al cabo, deseo que nuestra colaboración sea un éxito.

Mr Jackson: Vamos a ver, si he entendido bien, ha habido problemas con el embalaje. ¿Se han dañado las máquinas en el viaje?

Señorita Martín: No todas, solamente una. Pero el embalaje de otras tres está muy deteriorado. Parece que las cajas de cartón son demasiado frágiles.

Mr Jackson: Te aseguro que esto no volverá a ocurrir. Hoy mismo escribiré una nota a nuestro departamento de envíos. Tendremos que utilizar un embalaje mucho más adecuado para envíos al extranjero. ¿Qué otro problema ha sucedido?

Señorita Martín: Una de las impresoras no funciona bien. Hace un ruido tremendo.

Mr Jackson: Será mejor devolver la máquina defectuosa, así podremos examinarla a fondo en nuestro taller.

Señorita Martín: ¿Quieres decir que tendremos que esperar hasta que la máquina esté reparada?

Mr Jackson: ¡Claro que no! La cambiaremos por otra nueva. Te mandaré por entrega urgente una impresora nueva. La recibirás antes del fin de semana.

Señorita Martín: Otra cosa. El manual para el contestador automático no ha salido muy bien. La presentación y la tipografía están bien, pero la traducción es interminable y a veces muy difícil de comprender.

Mr Jackson:	¿De verdad? Bueno, si es tan mala, la tendremos que hacer de nuevo. Es muy importante que la traducción sea clara y comprensible. Antes de que volvamos a imprimirla, ¿puedes revisarla?
Señorita Martín:	¡Cómo no! Va en beneficio de todos. Me alegro de que hayamos llegado a un acuerdo tan rápido en todos estos puntos y espero que no tengamos más problemas de este tipo.
Mr Jackson:	Nos gusta tener satisfechos a todos nuestros clientes, dentro y fuera del país. No vaciles en llamarme si surge otro problema. Siempre tratamos de arreglar las cosas del modo más eficaz y con los menos trámites burocráticos posibles.
Señorita Martín:	Gracias, Peter, adiós.
Mr Jackson:	Adiós, Mercedes.

TRANSLATION

Señorita Martín:	Good afternoon. This is (*lit.* I am) Mercedes Martín of the company Ecofisa (speaking). I would like to leave a message for Mr Jackson. We have received the equipment (*lit.* equipments). Thanks for having sent it (*lit.* to have them sent) so quickly. Unfortunately it seems that there has been a small problem with the packaging. Can he call me at the office tomorrow, Wednesday, in the morning between eight and twelve if it (*lit.* to him) is possible? Many thanks.

Wednesday, 10.30 a.m. Mr Jackson rings Ecofisa.

Switchboard:	Ecofisa, hello.
Mr Jackson:	Good morning. I would like to speak to (*lit.* with) Miss Martín, please.
Switchboard:	Who's calling?
Mr Jackson:	Peter Jackson of Excel-Equip.
Switchboard:	Sorry (*lit.* excuse)! I can't hear you (*lit.* you I don't hear) well. Can you repeat your name, please?
Mr Jackson:	Jackson, J-A-C-K-S-O-N

Switchboard:	(Please) wait a moment ... . Mr Jackson? I'm putting you through now to (*lit.* now you I pass with) Miss Martín.
Señorita Martín:	Good morning, Peter. Thanks for calling me back (*lit.* to call me) so promptly.
Mr Jackson:	Not at all. It's the least (*lit.* that) I can do. I'm sorry that you have had some problems with the equipment which we sent you (*lit.* you have sent). What has happened exactly?
Señorita Martín:	Well, I don't think that they are insurmountable problems, but it is preferable to solve them as soon as possible, at least before the next shipment. After all, I want our working together to be (*lit.* that our collaboration be) a success.
Mr Jackson:	Let's see. If I've got it right (*lit.* have understood well) there have been problems with the packaging. Have the machines been damaged (*lit.* themselves have damaged the machines) in transit (*lit.* on the journey)?
Señorita Martín:	Not all (of them), only one. But the packaging of another three is very damaged. It seems that the cardboard boxes (*lit.* boxes of cardboard) are too flimsy.
Mr Jackson:	I assure you (*lit.* you I assure) that this will not happen again (*lit.* return to happen). This very day (*lit.* today itself) I will write a memo to our despatch department. We will have to use a packaging which is much more suitable for shipments abroad. What other problem has occurred?
Señorita Martín:	One of the printers doesn't work properly (*lit.* well). It makes a tremendous racket/noise.
Mr Jackson:	It will be best if you (*lit.* to) return the faulty machine, so we will be able to test it thoroughly (*lit.* examine it in depth) in our workshop.
Señorita Martín:	Do you mean to say that we will have to wait until the machine is repaired?
Mr Jackson:	Of course not. We will exchange it for another new one. I will send you by express (*lit.* urgent) delivery a new printer. You'll have (*lit.* receive) it by the weekend (*lit.* before the end of the week).
Señorita Martín:	Another thing. The manual for the answerphone hasn't turned out very well. The layout and the printing are fine, but the translation goes on and on (*lit.* is

never-ending) and (is) at times very difficult to understand.

Mr Jackson: Really? Well, if it is so bad, we will have to re-do it (*lit.* it we will have to do again). It is very important that the translation is clear and understandable. Before we reprint (*lit.* return to print) it, can you go over it?

Señorita Martín: Certainly! It's in all our interests (*lit.* it goes in benefit of all). I am pleased that we have reached agreement on all these points so quickly (*lit.* quick agreement on all these points) and I hope that we do not have (any) more problems of this sort.

Mr Jackson: We like to satisfy (*lit.* have satisfied) all our customers at home and abroad (*lit.* from within and outside the country). Don't hesitate to call me if another problem crops up (*lit.* arises another problem). We always aim to put things right (*lit.* sort out things) in the most efficient way and with the least red tape possible.

Señorita Martín: Thank you, Peter. Goodbye.

Mr Jackson: Goodbye, Mercedes.

Checklist 7

Masculine nouns:

el recado	message
el miércoles	Wednesday
el embalaje	packaging
el nombre	name
el envío	shipment, despatch
el éxito	success
el cartón	cardboard
el departamento	department
el ruido	noise, racket
el taller	workshop
el fin de semana	weekend
el manual	(instruction) manual
el beneficio	benefit, advantage
el acuerdo	agreement
el modo	way, manner
los trámites	red tape, formalities

Feminine nouns:

la mañana	morning
la caja	box

la nota	memo, note
la cosa	thing
la presentación	layout, presentation
la tipografía	printing, typing
la traducción	translation

Verbs:

dejar	to leave (behind)
perdonar	to excuse, pardon
pasar con	to put through (telephone)
mandar	to send
ocurrir	to occur, happen
desear	to want, wish
dañar	to damage
dañarse	to be damaged
suceder	to happen
funcionar	to work, function
devolver	to return (something)
examinar	to examine, test, go over
querer decir	to mean
salir	to go, come, turn out
imprimir	to print
revisar	to go over, check
alegrarse de	to be pleased
llegar	to arrive, reach
gustar	to please
esperar	to hope (You've already come across this verb meaning 'to wait for' and 'to expect'.)
vacilar en	to hesitate to
surgir	to arise, crop up
tratar de	to try to
arreglar	to arrange, sort out

Adjectives:

pequeño	small
posible	possible
alguno	some
insuperable	insurmountable
preferible	preferable
deteriorado	damaged, spoiled
frágil	flimsy, fragile
adecuado	suitable, appropriate
tremendo	tremendous
defectuoso	faulty
reparado	repaired, mended
urgente	urgent, express
interminable	never-ending, lengthy

malo	bad
importante	important
claro	clear
comprensible	understandable
satisfecho	satisfied
eficaz	efficient
burocrático	bureaucratic
amarillo	yellow

Adverbs:

desgraciadamente	unfortunately
pronto	promptly, quickly, soon
exactamente	exactly
solamente	only
a fondo	thoroughly, fully
a veces	sometimes
de nuevo	again

Prepositions:

antes de	before
dentro de	within, inside
fuera de	outside

Conjunctions:

hasta que	until, till
antes de que	before

Expressions:

quisiera	I would like
dígame	hello (on the phone)
de nada	not at all
lo mínimo	the least, the minimum
cuanto antes	as soon as possible
al menos	at least
al fin y al cabo	after all, when all is said and done
al extranjero	abroad
claro que no	of course not
salir bien/mal	to turn out well/badly
¿de verdad?	really?
volver a hacer algo	to do something again
¡Como no!	certainly!
ir en beneficio de	to be in the interests of

Irregular verbs:

oír ('to hear')
Present: **oigo, oyes, oye, oímos, oís, oyen**
Perfect: **he oído**
Present participle: **oyendo**

repetir ('to repeat')
Present: **repito, repites, repite, repetimos, repetís, repiten**
Perfect: **he repetido**
Present participle: **repitiendo**

salir ('to go/come/turn out')
Present: **salgo, sales, sale, salimos, salís, salen**
Perfect: **he salido**
Present participle: **saliendo**

sentir ('to be sorry', 'to feel')
Present: **siento, sientes, siente, sentimos, sentís, sienten**
Perfect: **he sentido**
Present participle: **sintiendo**

CHECKNOTES

66 Days of the week

The days of the week are normally written without a capital letter unless at the start of a sentence.

lunes	Monday
martes	Tuesday
miércoles	Wednesday
jueves	Thursday
viernes	Friday
sábado	Saturday
domingo	Sunday

The days are all masculine. Note that when we say 'on Monday', Spanish omits the preposition but puts in the definite article.

Example:

el martes	on Tuesday
los sábados	on Saturdays

67 Por la mañana ('in the morning')

Trabajo por la mañana en una oficina.
I work in an office in the morning.

Vemos la televisión por las tardes.
We watch television in the afternoons.

Siempre va al cine los sábados por la noche.
He always goes to the cinema on Saturday evenings.

BUT:

Son las ocho de la mañana.
It's eight in the morning.

68 The subjunctive

Study the following:

a) **Asiste a la reunión.**
   He attends the meeting.

   BUT

   Espero que asista a la reunión.
   I hope (that) he attends the meeting.

b) **Vds. escriben el informe.**
   You write the report.

   BUT

   Queremos que escriban Vds. el informe.
   We want you to write the report.

c) **El director no habla inglés.**
   The director doesn't speak English.

   BUT

   Siento que el director no hable inglés.
   I'm sorry the director doesn't speak English.

d) **Existen muchas oportunidades.**
   There are many opportunities.

   BUT

   Me alegro de que existan muchas oportunidades.
   I'm glad there are many opportunities.

e) **Exportamos más equipos a España que a Francia.**
   We export more equipment to Spain than to France.

   BUT

   Es importante que exportemos más equipos a España que a Francia.
   It's important that we export more equipment to Spain than to France.

f) **Habla español.**
   She speaks Spanish.

BUT

No creo que hable español.
I don't think she speaks Spanish.

In Spanish (and many other languages) certain verbs and expressions are followed by the subjunctive mood and this requires a change in the form of the verb that follows. For the moment, all you need to remember is that you should use the subjunctive in a subordinate clause introduced by **que** if the main clause expresses:

a) a hope
b) a wish
c) regret
d) pleasure
e) a value judgement (such as, 'it is important, better, normal')
f) uncertainty (such as, 'I don't think', 'I'm not sure')

69 The formation of the subjunctive

Take the 1st person singular (the 'I' form) of the present tense, remove the '**o**', and add . . .

. . . for **-AR** verbs like **compr-AR** 'to buy'	. . . for **-ER** and **-IR** verbs like **com-ER** 'to eat', **viv-IR** 'to live'	
compr- e	com- a	viv- a
compr- es	com- as	viv- as
compr- e	com- a	viv- a
compr- emos	com- amos	viv- amos
compr- éis	com- áis	viv- áis
compr- en	com- an	viv- an

There are, of course, some irregulars:

ser ('to be') **sea, seas, sea, seamos, seáis, sean**
ir ('to go') **vaya, vayas, vaya, vayamos, vayáis, vayan**
estar ('to be') **esté, estés, esté, estemos, estéis, estén**
haber ('to have') (auxiliary) **haya, hayas, haya, hayamos, hayáis,
hayan**

Examples:

Espero que estés bien.
I hope you are well.

No creo que vaya a reservar el hotel.
I don't think he is going to book the hotel.

Es importante que hables con el director.
It's important you talk to the director.

Se alegra de que hayamos llegado a un acuerdo.
He is glad we have reached an agreement.

Stem-changing verbs:

All **-AR** and **-ER** stem-changing verbs and those **-IR** verbs with 'e to ie' changes follow a similar pattern to the present tense, but with the subjunctive endings, like:

cerrar ('to close')	**cierre, cierres, cierre,**
	cerremos, cerréis, cierren
poder ('to be able')	**pueda, puedas, pueda,**
	podamos, podáis, puedan
divertirse ('to enjoy oneself')	
	me divierta, te diviertas, se divierta,
	nos divertamos, os divertáis, se diviertan

Stem-changing **-IR** verbs (e → i) retain the change throughout the conjugation in the subjunctive, like this:

pedir ('to ask for')	**pida, pidas, pida,**
	pidamos, pidáis, pidan

Stem-changing **-IR** verbs (o → ue) take the following pattern:

dormir ('to sleep')	**duerma, duermas, duerma,**
	durmamos, durmáis, duerman

Here are some examples:

Siento que no puedas pasar el día aquí.
I'm sorry you can't spend the day here.

Esperamos que durmáis bien.
We hope you sleep well.

Remember that some verbs have irregular 1st person singular forms (i.e. **tengo, veo, digo**), and these will form the base for the subjunctive, as in the following:

	1st person:	subjunctive:
tener ('to have')	**tengo**	**tenga, tengas,** etc.
disminuir ('to decrease')	**disminuyo**	**disminuya, disminuyas,** etc.
conocer ('to know')	**conozco**	**conozca, conozcas,** etc.
decir ('to say, tell')	**digo**	**diga, digas,** etc.

Examples:

Quiero que le digas la verdad.
I want you to tell him the truth.
Esperamos que tengan mucho éxito.
We hope you are very successful.

Some verbs go through a little spelling change just to keep the original sound of the verb:

Examples:

Quieren que organicemos una campaña.
They want us to organize a campaign.
La compañía espera que Vds. se encarguen del servicio postventa.
The company hopes that you are in charge of the after-sales service.
¿Quieres que te lo explique todo?
Do you want me to explain it all to you?

NOTE: If the subject of the dependent verb is the same as that of the main verb, we use the infinitive, not the subjunctive.

Compare:

Quiero enviar un paquete.	I want to send a parcel.
Quiero que mandes un paquete.	I want you to send a parcel.

70 Subjunctive after certain conjunctions

The conjunctions **antes de que** ('before') and **hasta que** ('until') usually take the subjunctive. Study the following:

Quiero terminar el informe antes de que lo leas.
I want to finish the report before you read it.

Empezarán la reunión antes de que volvamos.
They'll begin the meeting before we get back.

No hablaré con el director hasta que me mandes los resultados.
I won't talk to the director until you send me the results.

No podremos mejorar nuestras tasas de crecimiento hasta que el mercado se haga más favorable.
We won't be able to improve our growth rate until the market becomes more favourable.

71 The imperative

The subjunctive comes into its own again with polite only affirmative and all negative commands. (We'll leave the familiar affirmative commands for Unit 10 Checknote 107.) For example:

Using **usted**:

¡Abra las cartas!
Open the letters!

Vaya al banco.
Go to the bank.

Using **ustedes**:

Por favor, hablen más lentamente.
Please speak more slowly.

Vuelvan mañana.
Come back tomorrow.

Negatives:

No abras la carta.
Don't open the letter.

No llaméis antes de las once.
Don't phone before eleven o'clock.

No cambie el dinero en ese banco.
Don't change the money in that bank.

No manden los equipos.
Don't send the equipment.

When you want to use an imperative with pronouns, the rule is quite simple. Tag the pronouns (whether direct or indirect object or reflexive) on to the end of affirmative commands (and remember sometimes you will need to add an accent in order to maintain the original pronunciation), like this:

Hágalo.	Do it.
Explíquemelo.	Explain it to me.
Levántense.	Get up.

With negative commands, the pronouns precede the verb, like this:

No me llames mañana	Don't phone me tomorrow
No lo comas	Don't eat it
No me lo enseñe	Don't show me it
No te sientes allí	Don't sit there

72 Dígame

This word literally means 'tell me', and it is used when answering the telephone and is equivalent to 'hello'.

73 Volver a hacer algo ('to do something again')

Volver means 'to return', 'to go back', for example:

Vuelven a la oficina.   They go back to the office.

Volver + a + verb infinitive is a neat way of indicating the action is being repeated. For example:

Vuelvo a escribir el informe.
I'm writing the report again.

Han vuelto a hablar con el director.
They have spoken to the director again.

Va a volver a llamarte mañana.
She's going to 'phone you again tomorrow.

74 Devolver ('to return, hand back')

Devolver means 'to return something', 'to give/hand back' and shouldn't be confused with **volver** ('to return, come/go back'). For example:

Devuelvo el libro.   I return (hand back) the book.
¡Devuélvame la carta!   Give me back the letter!
Vuelve mañana.   He's coming back tomorrow.

75 Salir ('to go/come/turn out, leave')

The verb **salir** has slight changes in meaning depending on the context.

Examples:

Juan sale mucho.
John goes out a lot.

María sale de la oficina.
Mary leaves (*lit.* comes/goes out of) the office.

Los resultados han salido muy favorables.
The results have turned out very favourable.

El programa va a salir mal.
The programme is going to turn out badly.

76 Dejar ('to leave (something behind)')

Don't confuse **dejar** with **salir**. Study these examples:

He dejado el informe en mi despacho.
I have left the report in my office.

Salgo de la oficina a las cinco.
I leave (*lit.* go out of) the office at five o'clock.

77 Gustar (*lit.* 'to please')

In English we translate this verb as 'to like' or 'to be keen on', but in Spanish it means literally 'to please' so the object in English becomes the subject of the verb in Spanish, like this:

Me gusta el té.
I like tea (*lit.* tea pleases me)

Nos gustan los diseños.
We like the designs (*lit.* the designs please us).

No les gustan nuestras ideas.
They don't like our ideas (*lit.* our ideas don't please them).

If the phrase includes a noun, the indirect object pronoun is still included:

A María le gusta el trabajo.
Mary likes the work (*lit.* the work pleases her/Mary)

When the subject of **gustar** is a verb, the infinitive is always used in Spanish:

No me gusta trabajar.
I don't like working. (*lit.* to work doesn't please me)

Al señor Jackson le gusta vivir en las afueras.
Mr Jackson likes living on the outskirts. (*lit.* to live on the outskirts
    pleases him/Mr Jackson).

78 No le oigo bien ('I can't hear you well')

With verbs of perception ('hear', 'understand', 'see') 'can' or 'can't' is not translated:

Lo veo desde aquí.
I can see it from here.

No lo comprende.
She can't understand it.

79 Por and para

These two prepositions are sometimes confusing since they can both mean 'for' in English. Here are some guidelines to help you:

Por is used to indicate means, motive and exchange, and may translate as 'by', 'through', 'because of', 'out of', 'for the sake of' and 'for':

Hemos mandado los materiales por entrega urgente.
We have sent the equipment by express delivery.

Todo el tráfico pasa por el centro.
All the traffic passes through the centre.

Llegarán después de las ocho por el tráfico.
They'll arrive after eight because of the traffic.

Lo hago por necesidad.
I do it out of necessity.

Lo hace por su reputación.
She does it for the sake of his reputation.

Gracias por su carta.
Thanks for your letter.

Por is also used in the following expressions of time:

una vez por semana
once a week

por el momento
for the moment

por la mañana/tarde/noche
in the morning/afternoon/evening/night

Para is used to indicate purpose, suitability or destination, and may translate as 'to', 'in order to', 'so as to' and 'for':

Llama para hablar con la señorita Martín.
He's calling to speak to Miss Martín.

Van a abrir una oficina en Madrid para poder vender sus productos en España.
They are going to open an office in Madrid in order to be able to sell their products in Spain.

Fabricamos nuevos productos para hacernos más competitivos.
We manufacture new products so as to become more competitive.

una carta para el director
a letter for the director

Hoy sale para Venezuela.
Today he leaves for Venezuela.

Los alquileres son demasiado altos para la mayoría.
The rents are too high for the majority.

Para is also used in time phrases to indicate the time at which something is due to take place or by which something is due to have ended:

Quiero reservar la comida para las dos y media.
I want to book the meal for 2.30.

80 Sentir ('to feel (sense)', 'to be sorry')

Vas a sentir el frío.
You're going to feel the cold.

Siento tener que decirte . . .
I'm sorry to have to tell you . . .

Siente que no puedas asistir.
He is sorry you can't attend.

Note:

Lo siento.
I'm sorry.

81 Otro ('another')

This word first introduced in Unit 3 is an adjective and must agree in gender and number with the noun.

Examples:

otra dificultad
another difficulty (Note: no indefinite article in Spanish)

otras tres máquinas
another three machines

los otros mercados
the other markets

82 Todo ('all', 'every')

This adjective also first introduced in Unit 3 is used like this:

toda Europa	all Europe
todo el país	all the country/the whole country
toda la mañana	all morning
todos los días	every day
todas las compañías	every company/all the companies

83 Further uses of **ser** and **estar**

Ser tends to express an inherent characteristic or permanent state:

Soy el señor Jackson.
I'm Mr Jackson.

Son ingleses.
They're English.

El embalaje es demasiado frágil.
The packaging is too flimsy.

El trabajo será difícil.
The work will be difficult.

Son las ocho.
It's eight o'clock.

Estar tends to express temporary states and conditions, and also location:

El embalaje está deteriorado.
The packaging is damaged.

La máquina está reparada.
The machine is repaired.

Está mejor hoy.
She is better today.

¿Dónde has estado?
Where have you been?

84 Telephoning in Spanish

Here are some more useful expressions to use when talking on the phone.

Buenas tardes, soy Peter Jackson de la compañía Excel-Equip.
Good afternoon, my name is Peter Jackson of Excel-Equip.

Quisiera hablar con la señorita Martín.
I'd like to speak to Miss Martín.

¿Está la señorita Martín, por favor?
Is Miss Martín there please?

¿Me pasa/pone con el señor Redondo, por favor?
Can you put me through to Mr Redondo, please?

Llamo desde Inglaterra.
I'm calling from England.

Volveré a llamar más tarde/esta tarde/mañana.
I'll call back later/this afternoon/tomorrow.

¿Puedo dejarle un recado?
Can I leave him/her a message?

¿A qué hora estará de vuelta?
What time will she/he be back?

Possible replies from the Spanish secretary:

¿De parte de quién?
Who's calling?

¿Ya se ha puesto en contacto con él/ella?
Have you already been in contact with him/her?

¿Cómo se escribe?
How do you spell it?

Ahora le paso con ...
I'm putting you through to ... now.

Lo siento. No está en este momento.
I'm sorry. He/she is not here at the moment.

Now some excuses:

No está libre.
He/she isn't free.

Acaba de salir de la oficina.
He/she has just gone out of the office.

Está en una reunión.
He/she is in a meeting.

Está de vacaciones.
He/she is on holiday.

¿Quiere dejar un recado?
Would you like to leave a message?

¿Puede volver a llamarle esta tarde?
Can you ring back this afternoon?

Comprehension Practice 7

¿verdadero o falso?

1 La señorita Martín quiere que el señor Jackson le llame el jueves por la tarde.

2 Todos los equipos han llegado en buenas condiciones.

3 La señorita Martín desea que la compañía Excel-Equip solucione el problema cuanto antes.

4 El señor Jackson no quiere que el problema se repita y ya ha escrito una nota a su departamento de envíos.

5 Uno de los contestadores no funciona bien.

6 Excel-Equip va a examinar la máquina defectuosa en su taller.

7 La señorita Martín dice que revisará la nueva traducción del manual.

8 El señor Jackson siente que no hayan llegado a un acuerdo más rápidamente.

9 Excel-Equip siempre trata de tener satisfechos a todos sus clientes.

10 El señor Jackson sabe que es importante que Excel-Equip arregle las cosas del modo más eficaz.

FLUENCY PRACTICE 40

New words:

las vacaciones	holidays
pasar	to spend (time)
Polonia	Poland
asiático	Asian

You make your views known in response to a colleague's comments. Look at the example, and use the cues to express your point of view.

Example:

Voy a escribirle una carta.
(better/send a fax)
Es mejor que envíes un fax.

1 Pienso pasar mis vacaciones en los Estados Unidos.
   (better/spend them in Spain)
2 Voy al banco esta tarde.
   (important/go a.s.a.p.)
3 Juan volverá a la oficina a las cuatro.
   (important/return now)
4 Vamos a estar en Madrid el lunes.
   (better/be there Friday)
5 La compañía va a exportar a Polonia.
   (more important/export to Asian countries)

FLUENCY PRACTICE 41

New words:

ingresar	to pay in
el cheque	cheque
echar (una carta)	to post (a letter)
certificado	registered (mail)
el bocadillo	sandwich
la habitación	room, bedroom
informar	to inform
de	about
preparar	to prepare
distribuir	to distribute (like **disminuir**)

You're a bit of a taskmaster! Working in your Spanish office, you go through quite a list of jobs for your assistant. Use the imperative to issue your instructions. Follow the example:

Write a letter to Mr Guerra.
Escriba una carta al Sr Guerra.

1 Go to the bank and pay in these cheques.
2 Post this letter: send it registered.
3 Buy me some sandwiches at the bar.
4 Phone the Hotel Continental in Madrid and book a room for tomorrow.
5 Write a fax to Miss Martín in Madrid informing her of my visit.
6 Prepare these reports for the meeting.
7 Don't distribute them until I have seen them.
8 Go with Mrs López to reception and arrange the meeting with Mr González.

9 Go up to the fourth floor and deliver these documents.
10 That's all, thanks. Oh, and don't delay. We've got lots of work.

FLUENCY PRACTICE 42

New words:

el vuelo	flight
el apellido	surname

You have a meeting arranged for Wednesday afternoon with one of the directors of the Chamber of Commerce in Madrid. However your flight plans have had to be changed and you need to re-arrange the meeting. You telephone and speak to her secretary.

Secretaria: **Sí, dígame.**

You: Good morning. I'm John Cartwright, Sales Manager for the British company Euroquip. Can I speak to Mrs Redondo, please?

Secretaria: **Lo siento, pero la señora Redondo está en una reunión en este momento. ¿Quiere dejarle un recado?**

You: Yes, please. I have an appointment with Mrs Redondo for next Wednesday at 3.30, but unfortunately I have had to change my flight and I won't now arrive in Madrid until 4 pm. Will it be possible to see Mrs Redondo on Thursday morning?

Secretaria: **Un momento. El jueves por la mañana es imposible. La señora Redondo va a estar fuera de la oficina toda la mañana, pero Vd. puede verla por la tarde. ¿Le parece bien?**

You: Yes, of course. At what time?

Secretaria: **¿Puede venir a las cinco?**

You: Sorry, I can't hear you very well, what time?

Secretaria: **A las cinco.**

You: Yes, that's fine. Thank you.

Secretaria: **Y su apellido es Carter, ¿verdad?**

You: No, no. Es Cartwright, C-A-R-T-W-R-I-G-H-T.

Secretaria: **Gracias.**

You: Goodbye and thank you.

FLUENCY PRACTICE 43

Use the correct part of **ser** or **estar** to complete each sentence:

1 El señor Jackson / inglés.
2 El trabajo va a / muy difícil.
3 La fábrica / situada en el centro.
4 Ahora no / el momento oportuno.
5 Los resultados / muy buenos.
6 Creo que el director / libre ahora.
7 Nosotros / muy optimistas.
8 Vamos a / en Madrid mañana.
9 Espero que la máquina no / deteriorada.
10 Nuestros clientes / muy conservadores.

FLUENCY PRACTICE 44

New words:

el tren	train
el cine	cinema
el/la turista	tourist
las aduanas	customs

Complete the following sentences by replacing the asterisks with either **por** or **para**:

1 Trabajo en la oficina ** la mañana.
2 Quiero una habitación ** esta noche.
3 El tren ** Madrid sale a las tres.
4 ** el momento, está libre.
5 He mandado la carta ** fax.
6 Escribe ** confirmar la visita.
7 Sale al cine los sábados ** la noche.
8 Los turistas tienen que pasar ** las aduanas.
9 El mercado internacional es demasiado competitivo ** las pequeñas compañías.
10 Gracias ** haber distribuido los documentos.

FLUENCY PRACTICE 45

New words:

estar en huelga	to be on strike
efectuar	to effect, realize, bring about

Mr Jackson receives the following telex from Ecofisa's assistant manager:

345678	EXEQUIP L
876543	ECOFISA M

TLX NO. 4321   27-09-93   13.30

ATN: SR PETER JACKSON
REF: ENVIO DE IMPRESORAS

ROGAMOS ENVIEN URGENTEMENTE LAS IMPRESORAS YA QUE TENEMOS CLIENTES ESPERANDO.

AGRADECEMOS EL ENVIO TAN RAPIDO DE LOS NUEVOS MANUALES. LA TRADUCCION NOS PARECE BIEN.

SALUDOS CORDIALES

FRANCISCO GARCIA
GERENTE AUXILIAR

345678	EXEQUIP L
876543	ECOFISA M

Can you send a telex replying on behalf of Mr Jackson and include the following details?

- thank him for the telex
- you are pleased that the translation is okay
- you are sorry that they haven't received the printers
- the problem is that the British customs are on strike
- you assure him that you are doing all you can to effect delivery
- you hope to have better news tomorrow
- sign off

Spanish telephone company.

Applying for a job in Spain

This unit goes on to cover the conditional tense and further use of the subjunctive. At the same time, we aim to extend your knowledge of useful words and phrases associated with the theme of job applications.

Mr Jackson has been thinking for some time now about the possibility of living and working permanently in Spain. He's therefore very interested when he comes across an advertisement in a Spanish newspaper that might well suit him. Here is the advertisement:

M A R K E T O F I S A

EMPRESA LÍDER EN TECNOLOGÍA Y OFIMÁTICA

Necesita para sus oficinas centrales en Madrid

DIRECTOR DE VENTAS   7.500.000 pesetas negociables

Dependiendo del Director Gerente, se responsabilizará de todos los aspectos en el área: la comercialización y venta de los productos y servicios de la empresa en el mercado europeo, la definición de objetivos, política comercial y planes de marketing, la implementación de iniciativas, estudios del mercado, captación de clientes, etc.

SE REQUIERE: Titulación universitaria
Experiencia de al menos 8 años en ventas
Dominio total del idioma inglés
Sentido de creatividad y responsabilidad
Gran capacidad de liderazgo
Dotes de organización y motivación de equipos

SE VALORARÁ: Conocimientos de una tercera lengua europea
Master o Diploma en Márketing y Ventas
Experiencia en el sector de la ofimática

SE OFRECE: Incorporación inmediata a una sólida compañía en expansión
Posibilidades de desarrollo profesional
Alta remuneración y atractivo paquete de beneficios

Las personas interesadas deberán enviar su historial profesional al **Apartado de Correos 29.999, 28045 MADRID** indicando en el sobre **la Ref. 5.111-A**

TRANSLATION

MARKETOFISA
LEADING COMPANY IN TECHNOLOGY AND OFFICE AUTOMATION
Seeks for their head offices in Madrid

SALES MANAGER   7,500,000 pesetas negotiable

Reporting directly to the Managing Director, you will be responsible for all aspects within this area: the marketing and sales of the products and serviices of the company within the European market, the setting of targets, sales policies and marketing strategies, the implementation of initiatives, market studies and expansion of our customer base, etc.

Qualifications required:

University degree
Experience of at least 8 years in sales
Complete command of English language
Sense of creativity and responsibility
Strong leadership qualities
Skills in organization and team motivation

It will be an advantage to have:

Knowledge of a third European Language
Masters or Diploma in Marketing and Sales
Experience in the field of office automation

WE OFFER

Immediate appointment to a well-established expanding company
Possibilities for professional development
Top salary with attractive benefits package

Those interested should send their curriculum vitae to **PO Box No. 29.999, 28045 MADRID**, quoting **Ref. 5.111-A** on the envelope.

Having studied the advertisement, Mr Jackson decides to apply for the position. He prepares his CV, and writes his covering letter:

PETER JACKSON
19 HUGO LANE
ORPINGTON
KENT BR7 ABC
ENGLAND

Orpington, 23 de noviembre de 1993

Apartado de Correos 29.999
28045 MADRID
Spain
Ref. 5.111-A

Muy señores míos:

Con referencia a su anuncio en EL PAÍS de fecha 16 de noviembre para el puesto de Director de Ventas en su empresa con base en Madrid, me dirijo a ustedes para presentar mi candidatura.

Actualmente trabajo como Director de Ventas en la compañía Excel-Equip (Londres). Llevo más de seis años con esta compañía y cuento con una experiencia muy amplia en los sectores de ventas, exportación e informática. Durante los últimos años he ejercido las responsabilidades de dirección y coordinación de un equipo profesional de vendedores.

En la actualidad vivo en Inglaterra pero tengo la intención de buscar un puesto profesional que me permita establecerme de modo definitivo en España. Mi madre es española y me considero bilingüe.

Creo que cumplo con los requisitos que Vds. exigen, y les adjunto mi curriculum vitae detallando mis estudios universitarios, así como mi carrera profesional.

Tendría mucho gusto en tener la oportunidad de proporcionarles mayor información sobre mis proyectos futuros y estaría disponible para asistir a una entrevista en Madrid si así lo desean.

En espera de sus gratas noticias, les saluda muy atentamente,

Peter Jackson

TRANSLATION

Dear Sirs,

With reference to your advertisement in EL PAÍS dated 16 November for the position of Sales Manager in your company based in Madrid, I wish to apply for the post. (*lit.* I am writing to you to propose my candidature).

At the moment I am working as Sales Manager for Excel-Equip (London). I have been with this company for more than six years and I have (*lit.* count with) a very wide experience in the sales, exports and information technology sectors. Over the last few years I have been responsible for (*lit.* exercised the responsibilities of) the management and coordination of a professional team of salespeople.

At present I live in London but my intention is to look for (*lit.* I have the intention of looking for) a professional post which will enable me to settle permanently (*lit.* of definitive way) in Spain. My mother is Spanish and I consider myself bilingual.

I believe I have (*lit.* comply with) the qualifications which you ask for and I enclose my curriculum vitae giving details of (*lit.* detailing) my university education (*lit.* studies) as well as my professional career.

I would be pleased (*lit.* have much pleasure) to have the opportunity of providing (you) more information about my future plans and would be available to attend an interview in Madrid if you (*lit.* so) wish (*lit.* it).

I look forward to hearing from you (*lit.* In expectation of your welcome news)

Yours faithfully,

PJ

CURRICULUM VITAE

DATOS PERSONALES

Peter Jackson
19 Hugo Lane, Orpington, Kent BR7 ABC, Inglaterra
Teléfono: (07 44) 81 1234567
Fecha de Nacimiento: 31 de julio de 1960. Edad: 33
Nacionalidad: inglesa
Estado Civil: casado (tres hijos)

ESTUDIOS CURSADOS

1976: GCE 'O' Levels (equivalente BUP)
1978: GCE 'A' Levels (equivalente COU)
1981: BA (Hons) Economics (equivalente a Licenciatura en Ciencias Económicas) Universidad de Bristol.
1983: MBA (Master en Administración de Empresas) Universidad de Wisconsin, EE.UU.

IDIOMAS

Inglés-Español: bilingüe
Francés: excelente
Alemán escrito y hablado: buenos conocimientos

EXPERIENCIA PROFESIONAL

1983–84: Vicario-Muñóz S.L.
El Prat de Llobregat, Barcelona
(fabricante de productos electrónicos)
aprendiz
1984–87: Brown International Engineering Ltd, Londres
(maquinaria agrícola)
Gerente auxiliar, departamento de exportación
1988–90: Excel-Equip (London) Ltd, Londres
(ofimática)
Subdirector de Ventas
1990–9_: Excel-Equip (London) Ltd, Londres
(ofimática)
Director de Ventas

INTERESES PERSONALES

Artes marciales japonesas – judo y kárate
Paracaidismo
Música

OBJETIVOS

Utilizar mi experiencia profesional, mis relaciones con el extranjero y buenas cualidades de comunicación y liderazgo en beneficio del desarrollo comercial de Marketofisa.

REFERENCIA

Sr D. John Jones
Director Gerente
Excel-Equip (Londres)

Checklist 8

Masculine nouns:

Correos	Post Office
el anuncio	advertisement
el puesto	post
el equipo	team
el vendedor	salesman
el requisito	requirement, qualification
el curriculum vitae	CV, résumé
el gusto	pleasure
el proyecto	plan
el dato	fact, piece of information
los datos	data, information
el teléfono	telephone
el nacimiento	birth
el hijo	child, son
el estado	state
el bachillerato	secondary education studies leading to school-leaving qualification/matriculation
el conocimiento	knowledge
el fabricante	manufacturer
el aprendiz	trainee
el gerente	manager
el interés	interest
el judo	judo
el kárate	karate
el paracaidismo	parachuting
el liderazgo	leadership
el director gerente	managing director

Feminine nouns:

la referencia	reference
la fecha	date
la base	base
la candidatura	candidature
la experiencia	experience
la dirección	management, running
la coordinación	coordination
la actualidad	present, present time
la madre	mother
la carrera	career
la entrevista	interview
la edad	age
la nacionalidad	nationality

la licenciatura	degree
la universidad	university
la ciencia	science
Las Ciencias Económicas	Economics
la maquinaria	machinery
las artes	arts
la música	music
la relación	relation, relationship
la cualidad	quality, attribute

Months:

enero	January
febrero	February
marzo	March
abril	April
mayo	May
junio	June
julio	July
agosto	August
septiembre	September
octubre	October
noviembre	November
diciembre	December

Adjectives:

amplio	wide
profesional	professional
definitivo	definitive, final
universitario	of university
disponible	available
grato	pleasing, agreeable, welcome
civil	civil
casado	married
escrito	written
hablado	spoken
agrícola	agricultural, farming
auxiliar	assistant
marcial	martial

Verbs:

dirigirse	to direct oneself, write
presentar	to present, introduce, put before, propose
contar con	to reckon on, count, have (stem-changing o → ue)
ejercer	to exercise, perform
permitir	to enable, allow, permit

establecerse	to settle, establish oneself (like **ofrecer**)
considerar	to consider
cumplir con	to fulfil
exigir	to require, demand, ask for
adjuntar	to enclose
detallar	to detail
proporcionar	to provide

Preposition:

durante	during

Conjunction:

como	as

Expressions:

de fecha	dated
así como	as well as
tener mucho gusto	to have great pleasure
en espera de	awaiting, expecting,

Examinations:

BUP **Bachillerato Unificado y Polivalente** (school-leaving certificate, approximately equivalent to GCSE)

COU **Curso de Orientación Universitaria** (pre-university qualification approximately equivalent to 'A' levels)

Abbreviations:

S.L. = Sociedad Limitada   Limited Company
(**Vicario-Muñóz S.L.** = Vicario-Muñóz Ltd.)
S.A. = Sociedad Anónima   Limited Company
ECOFISA = Equipos de Oficina S.A.
          = Office Equipment Plc

CHECKNOTES

85 Conditional tense

In Peter Jackson's letter we find the following expressions:

tendría mucho gusto 'I would have great pleasure'
estaría disponible 'I would be available'

The verbs are in the conditional tense which translates into English as 'I/she/we etc/ would ...'

The conditional tense is formed by adding the following endings to the infinitive form of the verb, like this:

compraría	I would buy
terminarías	you would finish
vendería	he/she would sell
	you would sell
comeríamos	we would eat
abriríais	you would open
vivirían	they would live
	you would live

El programa incluiría todos los temas más importantes.
The programme would include all the most important topics.

Le gustaría verte.
He would like to see you.

No bebería el agua aquí.
I wouldn't drink the water here.

The endings are the same for all verbs, but there are some irregular verbs which have a different stem. Verbs which are irregular in the conditional are also irregular in the future tense which you've already met in Unit 6 (Checknote 58).

Here are some:

tener → **tendría**	I would have
hacer → **haría**	I would do, make
poder → **podría**	I would be able
poner → **pondría**	I would put
decir → **diría**	I would say
haber → **habría**	I would have (auxiliary)
salir → **saldría**	I would go out, leave

Tendría que mandar el cheque.
He would have to send the cheque.

¿Podría decirme ... ?
Could you tell me ... ?

Te lo habría dicho.
I would have told you.

And remember, the compound forms of these verbs will also be irregular:

Mantendríamos relaciones con las empresas extranjeras.
We would keep up contact with foreign companies.

86 Further use of the subjunctive

Study these sentences:

Conozco a una secretaria que habla español.
I know a secretary who speaks Spanish.

BUT

Busco una secretaria que hable español.
I'm looking for a secretary who speaks Spanish.

(Note that the personal 'a' is not required here because the person is not known or has not yet been identified.)

Tengo un trabajo que me interesa.
I have a job which interests me.

Quiero un trabajo que me interese.
I want a job which will interest me.

In the first sentence of each example the secretary and the post are known. When, however, there is uncertainty about the existence of someone or something, the subjunctive is used in the relative clause. Here are some more examples:

Utilizamos un embalaje que no es demasiado frágil.
We use a packaging which is not too flimsy.

Prefieren un embalaje que sea menos frágil.
They prefer a packaging which is less flimsy.

He encontrado un puesto que me permite trabajar en el extranjero.
I've found a post which enables me to work abroad.

Quiero encontrar un puesto que me permita trabajar en el extranjero.
I want to find a post which will enable me to work abroad.

While we're on the subject of the subjunctive, here are some more irregular forms which are quite commonly used:

saber ('to know')   **sepa, sepas, sepa, sepamos, sepáis, sepan**
ver ('to see')   **vea, veas, vea, veamos, veáis, vean**
dar ('to give')   **dé, des, dé, demos, deis, den**

Examples:

Quiero que sepas la verdad.
I want you to know the truth.

Nos ruega que le demos la oportunidad.
He asks us to give him the opportunity.

And don't forget some of the little spelling changes that occur in order to maintain the original sound of the verb, like the following:

coger ('to take')   **coja, cojas, coja, cojamos, cojáis, cojan**
empezar ('to begin')   **empiece, empieces, empiece, empecemos, empecéis, empiecen**

Examples:

Es mejor que cojáis el tren.
You'd better take the train.

Es imprescindible que empecemos a las ocho.
It's vital we start at eight.

Remember it is the first person singular of the present tense which gives you the stem for the subjunctive. Here are some irregulars to remind you:

salir ('to go out')
      → **salgo** ('I go out') → **salga, salgas, salga,** etc.
poner ('to put')
      → **pongo** ('I put') → **ponga, pongas, ponga,** etc.
hacer ('to do/make')
      → **hago** ('I do/make') → **haga, hagas, haga,** etc.

Examples:

Es mejor que salgas ahora.
You'd better leave now.

¡No lo hagas!   Don't do it!

Pónganos dos cervezas.
Give us two beers.

87 Más de ('more than')

In Unit 4 (Checknote 44) you learnt that **más/menos que** meant 'more/less than', for example:

Esta secretaria tiene más trabajo que aquélla.
This secretary has more work than that one.

Los sueldos en Inglaterra son más altos que los de España.
The salaries in England are higher than those in Spain.

When 'more/less than' is followed by a number the **que** changes to **de**, like this:

La empresa tiene más de doce sucursales.
The company has more than twelve branches.

Ha bebido más de ocho cervezas.
He has drunk more than eight beers.

Habrá menos de once personas en la reunión.
There will be fewer than eleven people in the meeting.

88 Position of adjectives

In the advertisement prepared by Marketofisa for a sales manager we met the following:

SE REQUIERE:	Titulación universitaria
	Dominio total del idioma inglés
REQUIRED:	University Degree
	Complete command of the English language
SE OFRECE:	Alta remuneración y atractivo paquete de beneficios
WE OFFER:	Top salary and attractive benefits package

You'll have noticed that the adjective is sometimes placed in front of the noun and sometimes after. The position of adjectives in Spanish is fairly flexible and is often determined by emphasis or style and with practice you'll soon overcome any initial difficulties. In fact, most adjectives come after, but here's a list of those which normally precede the noun:

a) adjectives of quantity:

bastante	enough
cuanto	how much
demasiado	too much
mucho	a lot of
poco	little
tanto	so much

Examples:

Han surgido demasiadas dificultades.
Too many difficulties have arisen.

No hay bastante trabajo.
There isn't enough work.

b) indefinite adjectives

alguno	some, any
cada	each
ninguno	none
otro	other
tal	such
todo	all

Examples:

Tomaré otra cerveza.
I'll have another beer.

Cada is invariable: **cada día** each day

Cada empresa importa productos diferentes.
Each company imports different products.

Tal is never followed by the indefinite article:

Va a ser imposible solucionar tal problema.
It's going to be impossible to solve such a problem.

No vamos a ir en tales condiciones.
We are not going to go in such conditions.

c) commonly used adjectives like:

pequeño	small
hermoso	beautiful
joven	young
viejo	old

Examples:

una hermosa vista	a beautiful view
un joven director	a young director

d) the following adjectives which, in addition, have a shortened
   form before a masculine noun:

bueno	**buen**	good
malo	**mal**	bad
alguno	**algún**	some
ninguno	**ningún**	none
primero	**primer**	first
tercero	**tercer**	third

Examples:

una buena idea   a good idea

Ofrecen (un) buen servicio.
They offer a good service.

Ha escrito su primer libro.
He has written his first book.

Son malas noticias.
It's bad news.

e) the following adjectives which have a shortened form before nouns of either gender:

grande	**gran**	big, great
cualquiera	**cualquier**	any

Examples:

cualquier tren	any train
cualquier persona	any person
Gran Bretaña	Great Britain
un gran cambio	a great change

f) Certain adjectives change their meaning according to their position:

una máquina nueva	a (brand) new machine
una nueva máquina	a new (different) machine
una señora pobre	a poor (not rich) woman
pobre Juan	poor (unfortunate) John
el mismo director	the same director
el director mismo	the director himself
una empresa grande	a big company
una gran empresa	a great company

89 **Agrícola** ('agricultural, farming')

This adjective does not have a masculine form:

trabajo agrícola	agricultural work
producción agrícola	agricultural production

90 Numbers

In Unit 2, you learnt numbers up to 29. Here are some more which you will need – try to learn as many as you can, and use this section to refer back to when necessary:

treinta	30	sesenta	60
treinta y tres	33	sesenta y seis	66
treinta y seis etc.	36	setenta	70
cuarenta	40	setenta y siete	77
cuarenta y cuatro	44	ochenta	80
cincuenta	50	ochenta y ocho	88
cincuenta y cinco	55	noventa	90
		noventa y nueve	99

Examples:

cuarenta y dos camareros
forty-two waiters

cincuenta y seis catálogos
fifty-six catalogues

You will remember that 'one' (**un/uno/una**) changed according to the gender of the noun. Similarly 'twenty-one, thirty-one, etc', agree in gender with the noun and become shortened before a masculine noun:

treinta y un años
thirty-one years

cuarenta y una señoras
forty-one ladies

¿cuántos años tiene?
how old is she?

tiene cincuenta y uno
she's fifty-one

cien	100
ciento dos	102
ciento sesenta y uno	161

Note that in English we put 'a' before the word 'hundred', but in Spanish this is dropped.

Examples:

Hay cien libros.
There are a hundred books.

Fabrican más de ciento veinte productos.
They manufacture more than a hundred and twenty products.

doscientos	200
doscientos veinte	220
trescientos	300
trescientos uno	301
cuatrocientos	400
cuatrocientos tres	403
quinientos	500
quinientos once	511
seiscientos	600
seiscientos ocho	608
setecientos	700
setecientos treinta	730
ochocientos	800
ochocientos ochenta	880
novecientos	900
novecientos noventa y nueve	999
mil	1000
dos mil	2000
tres mil cuatrocientos dos	3402

Numbers which finish in **-cientos** change according to the gender of the noun which follows.

Examples:

doscientos clientes
two hundred customers

trescientas cincuenta compañías
three hundred and fifty companies

BUT mil is invariable:

catorce mil pesetas
fourteen thousand pesetas

91 Dates

These are fairly straightforward in Spanish. From 2nd onwards the cardinal numbers are used, like this:

el primero de enero	1st January
el dos de marzo	2nd March
el quince de agosto	15th August
el once de octubre	11th October
etc.	

In Spanish we say the years like this:

1939 = one thousand nine hundred thirty and nine
= **mil novecientos treinta y nueve**
1990 = **mil novecientos noventa**
in 1820 = **en el año mil ochocientos veinte**

92 Contar con ('to rely/count/depend on', 'have')

Contar is a stem-changing **-AR** verb which, when used on its own, means 'to count, recount/tell':

Mi hijo sabe contar hasta veinte.
My son can count up to twenty.

Nos cuenta sus experiencias.
She tells us her experiences.

But **contar** used with the preposition **con** means 'to rely, depend or count on or have someone or something', for example:

El proyecto cuenta con muchas ventajas.
The project has many advantages.

Puedes contar con el director.
You can rely on the director.

No han contado con tales condiciones.
They haven't bargained on such conditions.

Comprehension Practice 8

Look back at the advertisement and answer these questions in Spanish:

1 ¿En qué se especializa Marketofisa?
2 ¿Dónde está la compañía?
3 ¿Qué busca la compañía?
4 ¿Cuántos años de experiencia deben tener los candidatos?
5 ¿De qué idiomas deben tener conocimientos?

Now, study again Mr Jackson's letter and CV and answer these questions:

6 ¿En qué sectores tiene mucha experiencia el señor Jackson?
7 ¿De qué nacionalidad es su madre?
8 ¿Desde cuándo está trabajando en Inglaterra?
9 ¿Qué idiomas habla?
10 ¿Qué le interesa hacer cuando no trabaja?

FLUENCY PRACTICE 46

New words:

la libra	pound (£)
el dólar	dollar ($)
la peseta	peseta (Spanish unit of currency)
el peso	peso (unit of currency of some Latin American countries, including Mexico)

Imagine you have to write out cheques for the following amounts:

a) £80

b) $23

c) £33

d) 47.000 pesetas

e) $503

f) 7.900 pesos

g) £448

h) $100

i) 58.700 pesetas

j) 35.846 pesos

k) £2.437

l) $371.000

m) 60.510 pesetas

n) £171

o) $626

FLUENCY PRACTICE 47

New words:

el coche	car
la puerta	door
la casa	house
el jardín	garden

In each of the following sentences substitute the infinitive in brackets for the correct part of the verb. You have to decide whether to use the subjunctive or not. Look back to Checknote 86 to remind you of the rule:

1 Hago un trabajo que no (**ser**) difícil.
2 Prefiero un coche que (**tener**) cinco puertas.
3 Necesitamos un director que (**saber**) hablar español.
4 Buscan un representante que (**poder**) desarrollar sus intereses en España.
5 Vivimos en una casa que (**gozar**) de un jardín estupendo.

FLUENCY PRACTICE 48

New word:

el médico	doctor

Here's some further practice with the subjunctive. In each sentence, select the appropriate verb and change the infinitive to the correct part of the verb. Don't forget some verbs are irregular:

1 Me alegro de que vosotros (**haber/ir**) a ir en coche.
2 Quiere que sus hijos (**coger/empezar**) el tren de las ocho.
3 Sentimos mucho que Vds. (**tener/haber**) tenido que hacer el trabajo.
4 Vamos a volver a casa antes de que (**empezar/ir**) el programa.
5 Es mejor que tú (**ver/hacer**) al médico hoy.

FLUENCY PRACTICE 49

Complete the following sentences by translating the verbs into Spanish using the conditional tense:

1 (He would have) mucho gusto en asistir a la reunión.
2 (I would like to) vivir en una casa grande.
3 (We could) venir mañana.
4 Ha dicho que (she would not do) el trabajo.
5 (It would be) mejor ir en coche.
6 Nos ha informado que el congreso (would finish) hoy.

FLUENCY PRACTICE 50

New words:

el mar   sea
la cartera   briefcase

Select an adjective from the list below which you think will fit into the gaps in the sentences. You'll also have to decide whether they go before or after the noun, and don't forget to make them agree with the noun:

grande	malo	tercero	mismo	pobre
nuevo	agrícola	hermoso		

1 Tenemos el ... problema ...
2 Han comprado un ... coche ...
3 Es una ... compañía ... con más de 20 surcursales.
4 Ha habido muchas dificultades en el ... sector ...
5 Desafortunadamente han ofrecido un ... servicio ...
6 Su oficina está en la ... planta ...
7 La casa tiene unas ... vistas ... al mar.
8 El ... señor ... ha perdido su cartera.

DICTIONARY PRACTICE 2

Study the following advertisement and with the help of your dictionary, answer the questions below:

SERRANO-HIGUERA S.A.
Selección de Directivos
DIRECTOR DE PROMOCIÓN

Nuestro cliente, compañía multinacional líder en el sector de la alimentación, dentro de un ambicioso plan de expansión, desea incorporar en sus oficinas de Barcelona, un Director de Promoción.

En dependencia del Consejo de Administración, se responsabilizará de apoyar e implantar ideas e iniciativas empresariales, definiendo y proponiendo objetivos y políticas comerciales. Asimismo será responsable del análisis global de los mercados con vistas a la captación de clientes y a la elaboración de nuevos proyectos.

El puesto está dirigido a un profesional con al menos diez años de experiencia en el sector de las áreas de Gerencia, Comercio o Promoción y Desarrollo de Proyectos Empresariales. Se valorará la titulación universitaria y formación complementaria de un Master en Administración o Empresariales. Imprescindible dominio del idioma inglés así como conocimientos de un tercer idioma europeo. Edad entre 35–45 años.

Es un gran reto profesional y se ofrece la incorporación inmediata a una prestigiosa entidad. Retribución atractiva y beneficios adicionales en función de la experiencia y valía aportadas.

Rogamos a los interesados envíen CV y fotografía a, **Serrano-Higuera SA – SELECCIÓN DE DIRECTIVOS – Paseo Marítimo 111, 08044 Barcelona**, indicando en el sobre la referencia **(ESA-1234)**

1 What post is being advertised?
2 What sort of company is Serrano-Higuera?
3 What field does the multinational company deal in?
4 Who will the new appointee be responsible to?
5 What will his/her responsibilities be?
6 In what areas should the candidate have some experience?
7 What qualifications are required?
8 Are languages a requirement or an advantage?
9 What factors will affect the salary offered?
10 What must interested candidates do?

142

Here is a much shorter job advertisement. Check that you understand what is required and what is being offered, and formulate questions to fill in any missing details you would need to know.

Empresa Aseguradora de Asistencia Sanitaria precisa para MADRID

Jefe de Ventas

✔ Experiencia Sector Seguros
✔ Edad 25-35 años.
✔ Se valorará titulación media o superior.

Ofrece:
✔ Retribución fija + incentivos.
✔ Seguridad Social.
✔ Incorporación inmediata.

Remitir "Curriculum Vitae" al Apdo. 53.259 Madrid.

The interview

> In this unit, we introduce you to another past tense, the preterite. Some further uses of the subjunctive, ordinal numbers and more time phrases are included. A lot of new vocabulary related to interviews is also given.
>
> Mr Jackson has been short-listed for the post of sales manager with Marketofisa and has arrived in Madrid for an interview with señora Vargas, head of Human Resources.

The Interview

Mr Jackson: Buenos días. Tengo una cita a las once y media. ¿Puede decirme dónde está el despacho de la señora Vargas?

In the interview room.

Sra Vargas: Buenos días, señor Jackson. Siéntese, por favor. Hemos estudiado su historial con interés y ahora nos gustaría hacerle algunas preguntas. Ante todo, ¿por qué ha decidido presentar su candidatura para un puesto en España? Después de todo, trabaja desde hace mucho tiempo en Inglaterra.

Mr Jackson: Hay tres razones principales: primero, siempre he querido establecerme en España con mi familia porque mi mujer es de Salamanca, mis abuelos son extremeños, y hemos mantenido estrechos vínculos con España, así que tanto nuestros hijos como yo somos bilingües. En segundo lugar, este puesto con Marketofisa parece corresponder muy bien a mis objetivos profesionales, así como a mi experiencia. Y en tercer lugar, me interesan especialmente la dimensión internacional de su compañía y sus contactos con el extranjero.

Sra Vargas: Vd. habla de su experiencia. ¿Qué beneficios le ha reportado esta experiencia a nivel profesional y personal?

Mr Jackson: Pues, cuando terminé mis estudios en junio del 1983, enseguida empecé mi primer trabajo, en agosto del mismo año, en la compañía Vicario-Muñóz en Cataluña. Allí pasé catorce meses trabajando como aprendiz en su departamento de informática. Escogí la informática por interés personal, pero desde el punto de vista del trabajo ha resultado muy útil. Posteriormente ingresé en Brown International Engineering Ltd. en Londres.

Sra Vargas: ¿Por qué decidió volver a Inglaterra?

Mr Jackson: El puesto en Brown representó un ascenso bastante importante para mí, me dio la oportunidad de trabajar en equipo, participar en la gestión de un departamento y de tener más responsabilidad de establecer y desarrollar relaciones con clientes extranjeros. Dejé Brown voluntariamente para el puesto de subdirector de ventas en Excel-Equip y en el año 1990 me ascendieron a director, puesto que ocupo actualmente. En Excel-Equip he ampliado mis conocimientos en el campo de la promoción de ventas: soy responsable de motivar a un equipo de doce vendedores técnicos y este año, tengo que decir que, se ha notado un aumento considerable en las ventas, quizás como resultado del sistema de bonificaciones que establecí el año pasado. A nivel personal, he aprovechado la experiencia de trabajar con colegas sumamente profesionales que me han aportado mucho. Creo que esta formación es una base excelente para el puesto que Vds. ofrecen.

Sra Vargas: Sin duda, Vd. tiene buenas cualidades que le servirían en un puesto como el nuestro. ¿Podría hablarnos algo de sus puntos fuertes, y quizás de los débiles también?

Mr Jackson: Mis cualidades positivas, creo que son mi deseo de llevar a cabo mis proyectos, hacer progresos sin jamás arriesgarme demasiado. Sé analizar una situación y escoger el momento oportuno para ponerme en marcha, lo cual es importantísimo en el mundo comercial. Además, sé delegar mis responsabilidades y no me considero insustituible. Hago todo lo posible para crear un ambiente positivo en mi departamento. Por otra parte, de vez en cuando me han acusado de ser inflexible pero yo prefiero pensar que esta llamada inflexibilidad siempre ha tenido un propósito noble.

Sra Vargas: En su carta, Vd. no se refiere a su sueldo actual. Me imagino, sin embargo, que el sueldo que ofrecemos nosotros no significa un aumento importante para Vd., puesto que en general los sueldos en España suelen ser inferiores a los de Inglaterra. ¿Cuáles son sus pretensiones en cuanto a esto?

Mr Jackson: Reconozco que si logro este puesto, el aumento en el sueldo será, digamos, modesto, pero teniendo en cuenta el coste de vida y el hecho de que tanto mi familia como yo estamos muy entusiasmados con la idea de vivir en España, creo que las ventajas a largo plazo pesan más que los arreglos iniciales. En cuanto a su oferta, ¿sería posible aclarar algunos puntos en cuanto al paquete de beneficios?

Sra Vargas: ¡Claro que sí! El Director de Ventas así como la mayoría de nuestros ejecutivos dispone de un coche. A través de un sistema especial, todos nuestros empleados pueden participar de los beneficios de la compañía; consideramos que es un modo eficaz de aumentar la motivación y la productividad. Además, pueden optar por hacerse un seguro de vida, y contribuir al plan de pensiones de la entidad, el cual ofrece condiciones muy favorables. Otros beneficios financieros del paquete son un seguro privado de enfermedad, facilidades bancarias para obtener un préstamo hipotecario muy económico y otras ayudas económicas. Además del sueldo, en diciembre se da una paga extraordinaria, la cual es normalmente un porcentaje del sueldo anual, y una cesta navideña.

Mr Jackson: ¿Y se incluyen beneficios sociales en el paquete?

Sra Vargas: Sí. Gozamos de unas excelentes instalaciones deportivas, incluso, creo que ya existe un club de kárate, el cual seguramente le interesaría, ¿no?

	También tenemos un restaurante subvencionado, y hay un programa de actividades sociales durante todo el año para los empleados y sus familias.
Mr Jackson:	Me alegro. Creo que a mi familia le gustaría aprovechar tales facilidades para conocer a gente. A veces puede ser difícil adaptarse a un nuevo ambiente.
Sra Vargas:	Una última pregunta ... ¿estaría Vd. en condiciones de realizar frecuentes viajes de negocios? ¿Cómo se las arreglaría su familia?
Mr Jackson:	No hay problema. Mi mujer es muy independiente y ya está acostumbrada a que yo no esté siempre en casa. Por ejemplo el año pasado, salí de viaje en más de once ocasiones. A mi familia no le molesta que esté fuera, y por mi parte, me encanta la oportunidad de poner a prueba mis conocimientos lingüísticos y poder conseguir buenos resultados comerciales.
Sra Vargas:	Si le ofrecemos el puesto, ¿cuándo estará disponible para aceptarlo?
Mr Jackson:	Tendría que avisarles con tres meses de antelación.
Sra Vargas:	Bueno. ¿Quiere preguntar algo más?
Mr Jackson:	Sí, dos cosas más. ¿Cuánto tiempo dura el período de prueba? y ¿funciona un horario flexible en su compañía?
Sra Vargas:	El período de prueba es de tres meses, y por lo que se refiere al horario, estamos en vía de estudiar el asunto, pero aún estamos en la etapa de la planificación.
Mr Jackson:	Muy bien. Está todo claro. Gracias.
Sra Vargas:	Gracias, señor Jackson. Nos comunicaremos con todos los candidatos por teléfono durante la semana que viene. Gracias por haber venido a vernos. Espero que tenga un buen regreso a Inglaterra.
Mr Jackson:	Muchas gracias.

TRANSLATION

Mr Jackson: Good morning. I have an appointment at half past eleven. Can you tell me where señora Vargas's office is?

In the interview room.

Sra Vargas: Good morning, Mr Jackson. Sit down, please. We have looked at (*lit.* studied) your CV with interest and now we would like to ask (*lit.* make) you some questions. First of all, why have you decided to apply for (*lit.* present your candidature to) a post in Spain? After all, you have been working for a long time in England.

Mr Jackson: There are three main reasons: firstly, I have always wanted to settle in Spain with my family because my wife is from Salamanca, my grandparents are Extremaduran, and we have kept close links with Spain so that both our children and I are bilingual. Secondly, this post with Marketofisa seems to correspond very well to my career objectives as well as my experience. And thirdly, I am particularly interested in the international dimension of your company and its contacts with abroad.

Sra Vargas: You speak about your experience. What benefits has this experience brought you on a professional and personal level?

Mr Jackson: Well, when I finished my studies in June of 1983, I immediately began my first job, in August of the same year, with (*lit.* in the company) Vicario-Muñóz in Catalonia. I spent fourteen months there (*lit.* There I spent fourteen months) working as (a) trainee in their computer department. I chose computing out of personal interest, but from the point of view of work it has proved very useful. Subsequently I joined Brown International Engineeering Ltd. in London.

Sra Vargas: Why did you decide to return to England?

Mr Jackson: The job at Brown's represented quite an important promotion for me, it gave me the chance to work in (a) team, to participate in the management of a department and to have more responsibility for establishing and developing contacts with foreign clients. I left Brown's of my own accord (*lit.* voluntarily) for the post of assistant sales manager at Excel-Equip, and in 1990 they promoted me to manager, the post which I currently hold. In Excel-Equip, I have widened my knowledge in the field of sales promotion: I am responsible for motivating a team of twelve specialist salespeople and this year I have to say that we've noticed a considerable increase in sales (*lit.* a considerable increase in sales has been noticed), perhaps as (a) result of the bonus system I set up last year. On a personal level, I have profited from the experience of working with highly professional colleagues who have taught (*lit.* brought) me a lot. I think this training is an excellent basis for the post (which) you offer.

Sra Vargas: You have no doubt (*lit.* no doubt you have) good qualities which would be of use in a post like ours. Could you tell us something about (*lit.* speak to us something of) your strong points and perhaps your weak points too?

Mr Jackson: My positive qualities, I think, are my desire to carry through my plans, to progress without ever taking too many risks (*lit.* risking too much). I know how to analyse a situation and choose the right moment to act, which is very important in the world of business. In addition, I know how to delegate my responsibilities and I don't consider myself irreplaceable. I do everything possible to create a positive atmosphere in my department. On the other hand, I have been accused (*lit.* they have accused me) on occasions, of being inflexible, but I prefer to think that this so-called inflexibility has always been in a good cause (*lit.* had a noble purpose).

Sra Vargas: In your letter, you don't refer to your present salary. I imagine, however, that the salary which we are offering does not represent/mean a significant increase for you, since, in general, the salaries in Spain are usually lower than those in England. What are your requirements as regards this?

Mr Jackson: I know (*lit.* acknowledge) that if I get this job, the increase in salary will be, let's put it this way, modest, but bearing in mind the cost of living and the fact that both my family and I are very excited about the idea of living in Spain, I think that the benefits in the long term outweigh (*lit.* weigh more than) the initial adjustments. As regards your offer, could you (*lit.* would it be possible to) clarify certain (*lit.* some) points regarding the benefits package?

Sra Vargas: Of course! The sales director like the majority of our executives has (*lit.* at his disposal) a car. Through a special scheme, all our employees can share in the profits of the company; we consider this to be (*lit.* that this is) an effective way of increasing motivation and productivity. In addition, they can opt to take out life insurance, and contribute to the company's pension plan which offers very favourable terms. Other financial benefits of the package are private health insurance (*lit.*

private insurance for illness), bank facilities for obtaining a very inexpensive mortgage loan and other financial help. Over and above the salary, a bonus payment which is normally a percentage of the annual salary is made in December, along with (*lit.* and) a Christmas hamper.

Mr Jackson: And are social benefits included in the package?

Sra Vargas: Yes. We have excellent sports facilities, actually I think there is already a karate club which would no doubt interest you, wouldn't it? We also have a subsidized restaurant, and there is a programme of social activities throughout the year for employees and their families.

Mr Jackson: I am pleased. I think that my family would like to make use of such facilities to get to know people. Sometimes it can be difficult to adapt to a new environment.

Sra Vargas: One last question ... Would you be in a position to make frequent business trips? How would your family manage?

Mr Jackson: There's no problem (there). My wife is very independent and she is already used to me not being always at home. For example, last year, I went on trips on more than eleven occasions. My family doesn't mind me being away, and I for my part am delighted to have the chance (*lit.* the chance enchants me) to test my linguistic knowledge and to achieve good business results.

Sra Vargas: If we offer you the job, when will you be available to accept it?

Mr Jackson: I would have to give (them) three months' notice.

Sra Vargas: Fine. Do you wish to ask anything else?

Mr Jackson: Yes, two other things. How long is the trial period (*lit.* how much time lasts the trial period), and is flexitime in operation (*lit.* does a flexible timetable operate) in your company?

Sra Vargas: The trial period is for three months, and as regards hours, we are in the process of studying the matter but are still at the planning stage.

Mr Jackson: Fine. It's all quite clear. Thank you.

Sra Vargas: Thank you, Mr Jackson. We will be in touch with all the candidates by telephone during next week. Thank you for coming (*lit.* having come) to see us. I hope (*lit.* that) you have a good journey back (*lit.* a good return) to England.

Mr Jackson: Thank you very much.

Checklist 9

Masculine nouns:

el historial	CV, résumé
el abuelo	grandfather
los abuelos	grandparents
el vínculo	link
los hijos	children, sons
el lugar	place
el objetivo	objective
el contacto	contact
el extranjero	abroad
el nivel	level
el empleo	job, work, employment
el ascenso	promotion
el subdirector	assistant manager
el aumento	increase
el deseo	desire, wish
el progreso	progress
el mundo	world
el ambiente	atmosphere, environment
el propósito	purpose, intention
el sueldo	salary
el coste de vida	cost of living
el hecho	fact
el arreglo	adjustment, sorting out
el ejecutivo	executive
el empleado	employee
los beneficios	profits
el seguro	insurance
el plan	scheme, plan
el préstamo	loan
el club	club
el viaje de negocios	business trip
el período de prueba	trial period
el horario	timetable, hours
el horario flexible	flexitime
el asunto	matter
el candidato	candidate
el regreso	return (journey)

Feminine nouns:

la pregunta	question
la razón	reason
la familia	family
la mujer	wife, woman
la dimensión	dimension

la informática	computing
la gestión	management
la promoción	promotion
la bonificación	bonus
la duda	doubt
la situación	situation
la inflexibilidad	inflexibility
la pretensión	aim, requirement, claim
la oferta	offer
la motivación	motivation
la productividad	productivity
la vida	life
la pensión	pension
la entidad	company, firm, organization
la enfermedad	illness, sickness, disease
la facilidad	facility
la ayuda	help, aid
la paga	payment
la cesta	basket, hamper
la instalación	installation, facility
la actividad	activity
la prueba	test
la etapa	stage
la planificación	planning

Verbs:

hacer una pregunta	to ask a question
establecerse	to settle (like **conocer**)
mantener	to maintain (like **tener**)
corresponder	to correspond
reportar	to bring
escoger	to choose (like **coger**)
resultar	to prove (to be), turn out (to be)
ingresar en	to join
participar	to participate
ascender	to promote (stem-changing **e → ie**)
ocupar	to occupy, fill
ampliar	to widen
motivar	to motivate
notar	to note, notice
aprovechar	to make (good) use of
aportar	to bring, contribute
servir	to be of use, serve (like **pedir**)
llevar a cabo	to carry through
hacer progresos	to make progress
arriesgarse	to take a risk
analizar	to analyse

ponerse en marcha	to act
delegar	to delegate
crear	to create
acusar	to accuse
imaginarse	to imagine, suppose
soler . . .	to be in the habit of . . . (stem-changing o → ue)
reconocer	to recognize, acknowledge (like **conocer**)
lograr	to get, obtain, achieve, attain
pesar más	to outweigh
aclarar	to clarify
disponer de	to have, own, have at one's disposal (like **poner**)
participar de	to share, partake of
aumentar	to increase
optar por	to opt for
hacerse un seguro	to take out an insurance
contribuir	to contribute (like **disminuir**)
obtener	to obtain (like **tener**)
incluirse	to be included (like **disminuir**)
adaptarse	to adapt
estar en condiciones de . . .	to be in a position to . . .
arreglárselas	to manage
estar acostumbrado a . . .	to be used to . . .
molestar	to bother, put out, trouble
estar fuera	to be out of town, abroad, away (on a trip)
encantar	to enchant, delight
poner a prueba	to put to the test, test
aceptar	to accept
avisar	to notify, inform, tell
preguntar	to ask
durar	to last
funcionar	to be in operation, operate
comunicarse con	to be in touch with . . .

Irregular verbs:

conseguir ('to manage, obtain, get')
Present: **consigo, consigues, consigue, conseguimos, conseguís, consiguen**
Present participle: **consiguiendo**
Perfect: **he conseguido**

Adjectives:

medio	half
extremeño	Extremaduran
estrecho	close, tight
personal	personal

útil	useful
técnico	expert, specialist
considerable	considerable
fuerte	strong
débil	weak
importantísimo	very/extremely important
insustituible	irreplaceable
llamado	so-called
noble	noble, honest, upright
modesto	modest
entusiasmado	excited, keen
inicial	initial
especial	special
privado	private
hipotecario	of/concerning a mortgage
extraordinario	extra, supplementary
anual	annual
navideño	of/concerning Christmas
social	social
deportivo	sports, sporting
subvencionado	subsidized
frecuente	frequent
independiente	independent
lingüístico	linguistic

Adverbs:

ante todo	first of all, first and foremost
después de todo	after all
primero	firstly
en segundo lugar	secondly
en tercer lugar	thirdly
posteriormente	subsequently, later, afterwards
voluntariamente	of one's own accord, voluntarily
sumamente	highly, extremely, exceedingly
sin duda	undoubtedly, without doubt
quizás	perhaps
jamás	never, not ever
de vez en cuando	occasionally, from time to time
en general	generally
además	also, in addition, moreover
normalmente	normally
aún	still

Prepositions:

sin	without
además de	in addition to

Interrogative pronouns:

¿Cuánto?	How much?
¿Cuánto tiempo?	How long?
¿Por qué?	Why?
¿Cuáles?	Which? What? (see Checknote 105)

Proper names:

Salamanca	Salamanca (town in Spain)
Extremadura	Extremadura (region)
Cataluña	Catalonia (region)

Conjunctions:

porque	because
cuando	when

Possessive pronoun:

el nuestro	ours

Relative pronouns:

el/la cual	which, who, whom
lo cual	which

Expressions:

desde hace mucho tiempo	for a long time
a nivel personal	on a personal level
con antelación	in advance
para mí	for me
todo lo posible	everything possible
digamos	let's put it this way, for want of a better word
a largo plazo	in the long term
¡Claro que sí!	of course!
en casa	at home
el año pasado	last year
de viaje	on a trip
por mi parte	for my part
algo más	anything else
en vía de	in the process of
la semana que viene	next week

CHECKNOTES

93 Preterite tense

This tense is used to express a completed action or an action that took place within a definite period of time. It is translated into English by, for example, 'I went, you saw, she did, we played, you ate, they bought'.

Regular -AR verbs in this tense are formed by taking the 'stem' of the verb and adding endings, like this:

terminar 'to finish'

termin**é**	I finished
termin**aste**	you finished
termin**ó**	he/she finished
	you finished
termin**amos**	we finished
termin**asteis**	you finished
termin**aron**	they finished
	you finished

Examples:

Trabajé en Londres doce años.
I worked in London twelve years.

Entre 1986 y 1989 representó a una compañía inglesa.
Between 1986 and 1989, he represented an English company.

Regular -ER and -IR verbs are also formed by taking the 'stem' and adding on the endings. In this tense they share the same endings:

escoger 'to choose'

escog**í**	I chose
escog**iste**	you chose
escog**ió**	he/she chose
	you chose
escog**imos**	we chose
escog**isteis**	you chose
escog**ieron**	they chose
	you chose

decidir 'to decide'

decid**í**	I decided
decid**iste**	you decided
decid**ió**	he/she decided
	you decided
decid**imos**	we decided
decid**isteis**	you decided
decid**ieron**	they decided
	you decided

Examples:

Decidimos ir a España.
We decided to go to Spain.

Salió de la oficina a las once.
He left the office at 11.

Devolvieron los libros esta mañana.
They returned the books this morning.

94 The preterite tense of ir ('to go')

As in English, this verb has an irregular preterite tense. It tends to be used a lot so try to memorize it as quickly as possible. Here it is:

fui	I went	**fuimos**	we went
fuiste	you went	**fuisteis**	you went
fue	he/she went	**fueron**	they went
	you went		you went

Examples:

Fueron a Madrid.
They went to Madrid.

¿Fuiste en el tren de las ocho?
Did you go on the 8 o'clock train?

NOTE: This also happens to be the preterite tense of **ser** 'to be', for example:

Fue un día estupendo.   It was a great day.

95 The preterite tense of dar ('to give')

This verb too is irregular in the preterite tense and is formed like this:

di	I gave	**dimos**	we gave
diste	you gave	**disteis**	you gave
dio	he/she gave	**dieron**	they gave
	you gave		you gave

Examples:

Ya te di el libro.
I already gave you the book.

El camarero nos dio la cuenta.
The waiter gave us the bill.

96 The preterite tense of empezar ('to begin')

Since the letter 'z' does not appear before 'i' or 'e' in Spanish, the 'z' becomes a c in the first person singular of empezar, like this:

empecé	I began	empezamos	we began
empezaste	you began	empezasteis	you began
empezó	he/she began	empezaron	they began
	you began		you began

All verbs ending in -ZAR follow this pattern.

Examples:

Hoy almorcé en un restaurante.
Today I had lunch in a restaurant.

Empecé el trabajo el lunes.
I began the job on Monday.

Analicé la situación.
I analysed the situation.

97 Further uses of the subjunctive

Molestar ('to bother') is a verb of 'emotional reaction' similar to alegrarse de ('to be happy') (see Checknote 68) and requires the subjunctive in the dependent clause. Here are some examples:

Me molesta que me escriba esta carta.
I mind him writing me this letter. (*lit.* it bothers me that he writes me this letter.)

¿Te molesta que fume?
Do you mind if I smoke? (*lit.* Does it bother you that I smoke?)

The verbal expression estar acostumbrado a ('to be used to') also requires the subjunctive in the dependent clause:

Está acostumbrada a que su hijo siempre vuelva tarde a casa por las noches.
She is used to her son always coming home late at night.

Estamos acostumbrados a que hable mucho.
We're used to him talking a lot.

98 The verb soler

This verb, followed by an infinitive, translates as 'to be in the habit of', or as expressions 'usually', 'generally' or 'as a rule':

Suelo levantarme a las ocho.
I usually get up at 8.

Por las mañanas suelen bajar al bar a tomar un café.
In the morning, as a rule, they go down to the bar to have a coffee.

99 Los abuelos ('the grandparents')

Often the masculine plural not only denotes a group of males, but also a mixed group of males and females:

el abuelo	**la abuela**	**los abuelos**
grandfather	grandmother	grandparents
el hijo	**la hija**	**los hijos**
son	daughter	children
el padre	**la madre**	**los padres**
father	mother	parents
el hermano	**la hermana**	**los hermanos**
brother	sister	brothers and sisters

Examples:

Mis padres viven en Inglaterra.
My parents live in England.

¿Tienes hermanos?
Do you have brothers and sisters?

Tengo un hermano y dos hermanas.
I have one brother and two sisters.

100 Ordinal numbers

You will remember **segundo** 'second' and **cuarto** 'fourth' from Unit 1. Here are the others which you will need:

primero	first	**sexto**	sixth
segundo	second	**séptimo**	seventh
tercero	third	**octavo**	eighth
cuarto	fourth	**noveno**	ninth
quinto	fifth	**décimo**	tenth

Beyond the 'tenth', cardinal numbers are generally used:

el sexto mes	the sixth month
la página doce	the twelfth page

With titles and centuries, the numbers generally follow the noun:

Carlos V (quinto)	Charles V
Enrique VIII (octavo)	Henry VIII
Alfonso XIII (trece)	Alfonso XIII
El siglo IX (noveno)	The ninth century
El siglo XX (veinte)	The twentieth century

The ordinal numbers form their feminine and plural in the usual way:

la séptima habitación	the seventh room
los primeros vuelos	the first flights

Primero and **tercero** are shortened to **primer** and **tercer** before a masculine noun:

∍l primer catálogo	the first catalogue
el tercer libro	the third book

101 The time

We first introduced you to telling the time in Unit 2 (see Checknote 16). Here are more phrases that will enable you to be more precise:

... y media	'half past ...'
... y cuarto	'quarter past ...'
... y veinte	'twenty past ...', etc.

Son las cuatro y media.
It's half past four.

Te veré a las ocho y cuarto.
I'll see you at quarter past eight.

El tren llega a las nueve y diez.
The train arrives at ten past nine.

... menos cuarto	'quarter to ...'
... menos veinticinco	'twenty-five to ...'

La reunión empieza a las once menos cuarto.
The meeting begins at quarter to eleven.

Es la una menos veinte.
It's twenty to one.

102 La semana que viene ('next week')

The phrase **que viene** ('next') can be tagged on to most expressions of time, for example:

el lunes que viene	next Monday
el mes que viene	next month
el año que viene	next year

103 The verbal phrase **arreglárselas**

The verb **arreglar** means 'to arrange, settle, put right or mend', for example:

¿Has arreglado la cita?
Have you arranged the appointment?

Trató de arreglar el problema.
He tried to settle/put right the problem.

Acabamos de arreglarlo.
We've just mended it.

The reflexive verb **arreglarse** + **las**, however, means 'to get by, manage', and is used like this:

¿Cómo te las arreglas?
How do you manage?

A pesar de las dificultades, se las arregla muy bien.
Despite the difficulties, she manages very well.

104 Possessive pronouns

In the dialogue you will have noticed **señora Vargas** using the possessive pronoun **el nuestro** ('ours'). Here are the others:

Singular	Plural	
el mío, la mía	**los míos, las mías**	mine
el tuyo, la tuya	**los tuyos, las tuyas**	yours
el suyo, la suya	**los suyos, las suyas**	his, hers, its, yours
el nuestro, la nuestra	**los nuestros, las nuestras**	ours
el vuestro, la vuestra	**los vuestros, las vuestras**	yours
el suyo, la suya	**los suyos, las suyas**	theirs, yours

Possessive pronouns always agree in gender and number with the noun they replace. They are always preceded by the definite article, except after the verb **ser** when the article is usually omitted.

For example:

mi oficina y la tuya
my office and yours

unos productos como los vuestros
some products like yours

este libro es mío
this book is mine

105 Interrogative pronoun ¿cuál?

This pronoun means 'which?' or 'which one?':

¿Cuál de los catálogos vas a mandar?
Which of the catalogues are you going to send?

Hay cuatro candidatos, ¿a cuál prefieres?
There are four candidates. Which one do you prefer?

¿Cuál? should also be used to mean 'what' in sentences involving
what + to be + noun. For example:

¿Cuál es su apellido?
What is your surname?

¿Cuál es el problema?
What's the problem?

When more than one thing/person is referred to, use the plural
¿cuáles? For example:

¿Cuáles vas a considerar primero?
Which ones are you going to consider first?

¿Cuáles son los puntos más importantes?
Which/what are the most important points?

106 Relative pronouns

Cual ('which') can be used instead of **que**, particularly after a
pause in speaking and when wishing to emphasize. It is preceded
by **el, la, los las**, agreeing in number and gender with its
antecedent, for example:

He mandado la carta, la cual tardé mucho en escribir.
I've sent the letter, (the one) which I took a long time to write.

**Existen problemas específicos, los cuales llevamos años intentando
solucionar.**
There are specific problems which we have spent years trying to
resolve.

When the antecedent is not a noun but a whole sentence or an idea, **lo cual** is used:

Las aduanas están en huelga, lo cual me molesta mucho.
The customs are on strike, which inconveniences me a lot.

Comprehension Practice 9

¿verdadero o falso?   true or false?

New words:

el/la entrevistador-a	interviewer
la pérdida de tiempo	waste of time
el márketing	marketing
el día siguiente	the following day

1 A los entrevistadores les interesa mucho el curriculum del señor Jackson.
2 El señor Jackson busca un puesto en España porque su trabajo en Inglaterra ya no corresponde a sus objetivos profesionales.
3 Pasó más de un año en su primer empleo.
4 Considera que la informática es una pérdida de tiempo.
5 Aprovechó el puesto en la compañía Brown para desarrollar relaciones con clientes extranjeros.
6 Ingresó en la empresa Excel-Equip en el año 1990 como director de márketing.
7 Estableció un sistema de bonificaciones el año pasado.
8 Desde el punto de vista profesional, el señor Jackson cree que los años en los que ha trabajado con la compañía Excel-Equip le han aportado muchos beneficios.
9 Marketofisa ofrece a sus empleados un paquete de beneficios muy atractivo.
10 El señor Jackson cree que su familia no tendrá ninguna dificultad para adaptarse a una nueva vida en España.
11 Los viajes de negocios no representan ningún problema para el señor Jackson.
12 El señor Jackson quiere hacerles tres preguntas más a los entrevistadores.
13 En la compañia funciona un horario flexible desde hace tres meses.
14 La señora Vargas le va a comunicar su decisión por teléfono el día siguiente.

FLUENCY PRACTICE 51

New words:

adquirir	to acquire, gain (stem-changing i → ie, like **invertir**)
dirigir	to manage, lead, direct
laboral	working
catalán, ana (*f*)	Catalonian
las posibilidades de acenso	promotion prospects

Study again the main text of this unit and then play the role of Mr Jackson in the following interview:

Sra Vargas: **Buenas tardes, señor Jackson. Por favor, siéntese. Acabamos de estudiar su curriculum y ahora nos gustaría hacerle algunas preguntas. ¿Por qué decidió Vd. presentar su candidatura para este puesto?**

Mr Jackson: Well, I think that the job corresponds exactly to my career objectives and to my experience in this field. In addition, I am especially interested in the international dimension of your company.

Sra Vargas: **Vd. habla de su experiencia. ¿Podría decirnos qué beneficios le ha aportado?**

Mr Jackson: I've been able to gain the necessary experience to establish and develop contacts with foreign clients. I've widened my knowledge in the field of sales promotion and I am now used to managing a team of professional salespeople.

Sra Vargas: **¿Ha pensado Vd. lo diferente que puede ser trabajar en una empresa española?**

Mr Jackson: I know that there are differences in the working conditions and practices compared with British companies. After all, I worked for over a year in a Catalonian company. However, I hope to respond positively to those changes and adapt without problems.

Sra Vargas: **¿Y qué opina su familia?**

Mr Jackson: They are very keen on the idea of living in Spain.

Sra Vargas: **Bueno. En cuanto al sueldo, ¿cuáles son sus pretensiones?**

Mr Jackson: The initial increase in salary is modest, but the post offers promotion prospects and therefore I am willing to consider the matter in the long term. Could you give me more details about the benefits package?

Sra Vargas: ¡Claro que sí! Tenemos un sistema de participación de los beneficios de la empresa, seguros de vida, de enfermedad, pensiones excelentes, facilidades bancarias, así como beneficios sociales para nuestros empleados y sus familias.

Mr Jackson: It is a very attractive package.

Sra Vargas: Si le ofrecemos el puesto, ¿cuándo estará disponible para aceptarlo?

Mr Jackson: Normally, I would have to give them two months' notice.

Sra Vargas: Eso me parece normal. Bueno, ¿quiere preguntar algo más?

Mr Jackson: Yes, I have one question. Is flexi-time in operation in your company?

Sra Vargas: Sí. Acabamos de introducirlo, y por el momento funciona bien, pero estamos todavía en el período de prueba.

FLUENCY PRACTICE 52

New word: **ayer** yesterday

Complete the following:

1 (I left) mi cartera en casa.
2 (She wrote) el informe.
3 (I began) la reunión a la una.
4 ¿Les (did you give) los catálogos a los clientes? (Use **tú**)
5 (They finished) sus estudios en 1987.
6 Ayer, (he got up) tarde.
7 ¿Por qué (did you decide) no volver? (Use **vosotros**)
8 El año pasado, la compañía (exported) más productos a Europa que a los EE.UU.
9 ¿A qué hora (did you call)? (Use **usted**)
10 (He analysed) la situación y (chose) el momento oportuno para ponerse en acción.

FLUENCY PRACTICE 53

Complete the following questions replacing the asterisks with one of the expressions listed below:

1 ¿ ** no tomas la cerveza? – Porque no me gusta.
2 ¿ ** terminó la reunión? – A las ocho y cuarto.
3 ¿ ** pasaste en EE.UU? – Dos semanas.
4 ¿ ** de las habitaciones quieres? – La más grande.
5 ¿ ** ingresó en la empresa? – El año pasado.
6 ¿ ** realizaste tus estudios universitarios? – En Madrid.
7 ¿ ** es el mercado español? – Es muy complicado.
8 ¿ ** está haciendo? – Está escribiendo una carta.

¿A qué hora?   ¿Cómo?   ¿Cuál?   ¿Por qué?   ¿Cuándo?
¿Qué?   ¿Cuánto tiempo?   ¿Dónde?

Plano de Madrid (Centro Ciudad)

Mr Jackson will have used this map for his house-hunting.

Buying a house in Spain

> In this unit there are some more items of grammar, but the emphasis is on extending your comprehension and vocabulary.
>
> Mr Jackson and his family have now moved to Spain and are looking to buy a house. They have decided on a residential area on the northern outskirts of Madrid, and now arrive for their appointment with the estate agent, señora Robles.

Mr Jackson: Buenos días.

Sra Robles: Buenos días.

Mr Jackson: Llegamos un poco temprano ...

Sra Robles: No, no. Siéntense, por favor.

Mr Jackson: Bueno. Soy inglés y acabo de obtener un puesto con una empresa de Madrid. Esperamos fijar nuestra residencia en España dentro de unos meses y queremos comprar una casa en las afueras de la ciudad. La semana pasada hicimos un recorrido por varias zonas y creo que ésta es la que más nos gusta.

Sra Robles: Perfecto. ¿Ya tienen una idea del tipo de propiedad que quieren, de su ubicación y sobre todo de su precio?

Mr Jackson: Sí. Lo hemos considerado detenidamente. Mi mujer sabe exactamente lo que quiere – un chalet, preferiblemente no adosado, con cuatro dormitorios. Queremos un jardín, y claro, un garaje. No nos importa que sea nuevo o de segunda mano. Debe estar habitable inmediatamente, pues yo no soy aficionado al bricolaje. Tampoco tendré tiempo para hacer reformas.

Sra Robles: ¿Y cuál es su escala de precios?

Mr Jackson: Entre los 30 y 35 millones de pesetas.

Sra Robles: Tenemos varias propiedades que corresponden más o menos a lo que buscan y que están dentro de su escala de precios. Miren Vds.; he aquí algunas fotos con los detalles de cada propiedad y sus inmediaciones.

Mr and Mrs Jackson study the photos.

Mr Jackson: Vamos a ver. Mira, querida, este chalet tiene mucho atractivo. ¿Y no te gusta ése?, es encantador ¿no? y tiene alrededores muy bonitos ... con esos pinos detrás ... Oh, pásame aquella foto. Dime, ¿qué piensas tú ...?

Mr and Mrs Jackson continue to study the photos.

Some time later ...

Mr Jackson: Bueno, hemos elegido ... éste en la urbanización Monte Rozas con vistas a la sierra, luego el chalet que tiene el jardín muy grande con garaje para dos coches, y este otro que a lo mejor les gustará a los niños porque tiene piscina. ¿Podríamos ir a ver los tres en los próximos días? ¿Estas casas están habitadas actualmente?

Sra Robles: Sí, dos de ellas están habitadas, la tercera no lo está. Organizaré unas citas para los próximos días con los dueños y les comunicaré las horas. Tengo sus detalles. ¿Es ésta su dirección, y éste, su número de teléfono?

Mr Jackson: Eso es. Estamos en casa de unos amigos.

A week later ...

Mr Jackson: Fuimos a ver las tres propiedades. Después de mucho pensar nos gusta más el chalet que da a la sierra ... tiene algo. Tendremos que hacer alguna que otra reforma pero está habitable. Vale 34 millones pero podríamos ofrecer treinta y tres.

Sra Robles: Sí, siempre vale la pena intentarlo. Comunicaré su oferta al vendedor, y si la acepta, les mandaré un Contrato Privado de Compraventa. Les ruego que me lo devuelvan incluyendo los documentos necesarios, y su pasaporte o carnet de identidad. También deberán pagar un depósito inicial de un 10 por ciento del precio. ¿De qué manera se proponen financiar su compra? ¿Van a pagar al contado o van a pedir un préstamo hipotecario?

Mr Jackson: Dada la situación poco estable en cuanto a los tipos de cambio y de interés, no estamos totalmente convencidos de que un crédito sea la mejor opción. Ya hablamos con el banco y decidimos financiar la compra por nuestra cuenta. Todo está arreglado y ya se han transferido los fondos necesarios desde Inglaterra.

Sra Robles: Muy bien.

Mr Jackson: ¿Qué ocurrirá si tenemos que retirarnos por alguna razón personal o cualquier otro motivo?

Sra Robles: En ese caso, perderán el depósito que se pagará como indemnización al vendedor quien, en teoría, podría reclamar daños y perjuicios adicionales.

Mr Jackson: Y una vez firmado el contrato si otro comprador viene y ofrece más que nosotros, ¿el vendedor puede aceptar libremente su oferta y retirarse de nuestro contrato?

Sra Robles: Eso no debería pasar. El contrato es una obligación por las dos partes. Sin embargo, Vds. no tendrán garantía absoluta de que la propiedad vaya a ser suya hasta que se firme la Escritura.

Mr Jackson: Otra pregunta importante. ¿Cuál es el plazo normal entre la firma del Contrato y la de la Escritura?

Sra Robles: Depende de las partes. El banco tiene que concluir los trámites. Su abogado hará las investigaciones, y puede que ocurran pequeños retrasos, pero una vez que el notario tenga todos los documentos se puede firmar la Escritura. Normalmente se decide la fecha para la firma de la Escritura cuando se firma el Contrato de Compraventa. Puede ser cuestión de unos días, semanas o meses.

Mr Jackson: Volviendo al tema del pago, si he entendido bien, pagamos un depósito de un 10 por ciento al firmar el Contrato, y, ¿cuándo se paga el resto?

Sra Robles: El resto se debe transferir directamente a la cuenta del notario antes o en el momento de firmar la Escritura.

Mr Jackson: He oído decir que los gastos intermedios son muy altos en comparación con los de Inglaterra. ¿Cuál es el importe aproximado para una casa como la que queremos comprar?

Sra Robles: No hay tarifa fija, pero en general los derechos del notario son del orden de unas 40.000 pesetas, pero pueden ser más. Luego para los costes de inscribir la casa tampoco hay escalas de precio, pero suelen ser entre las 18.000 y 20.000 pesetas. El IVA, el impuesto relacionado con la compra de una propiedad que no es de construcción nueva, es el 6 por ciento del precio de la compra.

Mr Jackson: ¿Y una vez comprada la casa hay impuestos adicionales?

Sra Robles: Hay una contribución que se paga al Ayuntamiento, la cual cubre los gastos de los servicios municipales, por ejemplo, de la limpieza. Ésta se calcula según el valor de la casa, y es responsabilidad del dueño de la propiedad. Si la casa pertenece a una comunidad de vecinos, habrá una contribución anual que varía según el tipo de comunidad. Encima, claro, están los gastos normales, luz, gas, teléfono, etc.

Mr Jackson: Bien. Creo que tenemos toda la información que necesitamos por ahora. Esperaremos la decisión del vendedor, y entretanto nosotros prepararemos los documentos los trámites y para el depósito. Hablaré con nuestro abogado para que empiece a preparar sus investigaciones sobre la propiedad. Espero que no haya ningún problema inesperado como, por ejemplo, la construcción de una autovía cerca de la casa. Bueno, Vd. necesita el nombre de nuestro abogado, aquí lo tiene, y también el del banco a través del cual haremos el pago.

Sra Robles: Muy bien. Yo me comunicaré con su abogado en cuanto sepa si el vendedor ha aceptado su oferta o no. Pero antes, si tienen alguna duda, por favor pónganse en contacto con nuestra oficina.

Mr Jackson: Muchas gracias.

Sra Robles: A Vds., y adiós, señor y señora Jackson.

Mr Jackson: Adiós, señora Robles.

TRANSLATION

Mr Jackson: Good morning.

Sra Robles: Good morning.

Mr Jackson: We're (*lit.* we arrive) a little early ...

Sra Robles: No, no. Sit down, please.

Mr Jackson: Well. I am English and I have just got a job with a company in (*lit.* of) Madrid. We hope to take up (*lit.* fix our) residence in Spain within the (next) few months and we want to buy a house on the outskirts of the city. Last week we did a tour of (*lit.* through) several areas and I think this is the one we like best (*lit.* most).

Sra Robles: Perfect. Do you already have an idea of the sort of property (which) you want, its location/position and more particularly (*lit.* especially) its price?

Mr Jackson: Yes. We have thought it over at great length. My wife knows exactly what she wants – a house, preferably detached (*lit.* not semi-detached), with four bedrooms. We want a garden, and, of course, a garage. We don't mind if it's new or old (*lit.* second-hand). It must be habitable immediately, since I'm not much of a do-it-yourself enthusiast. Neither will I have time to do improvements.

Sra Robles: And what is your price range?

Mr Jackson: Between 30 and 35 million pesetas.

Sra Robles: We have a number of properties which fit in more or less with what you are looking for and which are within your price range. Look, here are some photos with the details of each property and its surroundings.

Mr and Mrs Jackson study the photos.

Mr Jackson: Let's see. Look, dear, this house has a lot of appeal. And don't you like that one, it's charming, isn't it? And it has a really pretty setting ... with the pine trees behind ... Oh, pass me that photo over there. Tell me, what do you think ...?

Mr and Mrs Jackson continue to study the photos.

Some time later ...

Mr Jackson: Well, we've chosen ... this one in the Monte Rozas (residential) development with views of (*lit.* to) the mountain range, then the house with the very big garden with garage for two cars, and this other one which the kids will probably like because it has (a) swimming pool. Could we go and see the three over the next (few) days? Are these houses occupied at the moment?

Sra Robles: Yes, two of them are occupied, the third isn't. I'll arrange some appointments for the next few days with the owners and let you know (*lit.* tell you) the times. I have your details. Is this your address, and this your telephone number?

Mr Jackson: That's right. We are staying with some friends (*lit.* we are at (the) home of some friends).

A week later . . .

Mr Jackson: We went to see the three properties. After a lot of thought (*lit.* much to think) we prefer (*lit.* like most) the house which looks out on to the mountain range . . . it has a certain charm. We'll have to make the odd improvement but it is habitable. It costs 34 million but we could make an offer of (*lit.* we offer) thirty three.

Sra Robles: Yes, it's always worthwhile trying (*lit.* it). I'll pass on your offer to the vendor, and if he accepts it, I'll send you a Sale Contract. Please (*lit.* I ask that you) return it to me along with (*lit.* including) the necessary documents, and your passport or identity card. You will also have to pay an initial deposit of 10 per cent of the price. How (*lit.* in what way) do you propose to finance the purchase? Are you going to pay in cash or are you going to ask for a mortgage (loan)?

Mr Jackson: In view of (*lit.* given) the unsettled (*lit.* not stable) situation of the exchange and interest rates, we are not totally convinced that a loan is the best option. We('ve) already talked with the bank and decided to finance the purchase independently (*lit.* on our own account). Everything is arranged and the necessary funds have already been transferred from England.

Sra Robles: Fine.

Mr Jackson: What will happen if we have to withdraw for a personal (reason) or any other reason?

Sra Robles: In that case, you will lose the deposit which will be paid as compensation to the vendor who, in theory, could claim additional damages.

Mr Jackson: And once the contract is signed (*lit.* Once signed the contract), if another buyer comes along and offers more than us (*lit.* we), can the vendor freely accept his offer and withdraw from our contract?

Sra Robles: That shouldn't happen. The contract is binding (an obligation) for both (*lit.* the two) parties/sides. However, you will not be absolutely sure (*lit.* have absolute guarantee) that the property will be yours until the Deeds are signed.

Mr Jackson: Another important question. What is the normal period between the signing of the Contract and that of the Deeds?

Sra Robles: It depends on the parties. The bank has to conclude the transactions (*lit.* formalities). Your (own) solicitor will make his searches and small delays can occur (*lit.* it can that small delays occur), but once the notary has all the documents, the Deeds can be signed. You normally decide the date for the signing of the Title Deeds when you sign the Sale Contract. It can be a matter of (some) days, weeks or months.

Mr Jackson: Going back to the question of payment, if I understand correctly, we pay a deposit of 10 per cent on signing the Sale Agreement, and when do we pay the rest?

Sra Robles: The balance should be transferred straight to the notary's account before or at the time of signing the Deeds.

Mr Jackson: I've heard (it said) that the transaction (*lit.* intermediary) costs are very high in comparison to those in England. What is the approximate total/amount for a house like the one we want to buy?

Sra Robles: There is no standard price, but generally speaking, the notary's fees are in the order of 40,000 pesetas, but they can be more. Then for the costs of registering the house there is no set scale either, but they are usually between 18,000 and 20,000 pesetas. VAT, the tax related to the purchase of a property which is not a new construction, is 6 per cent of the purchase price.

Mr Jackson: And once we've bought the house (*lit.* once bought the house) are there more taxes?

Sra Robles: There is a tax which is paid to the town hall which covers the expenses of the local services, for example, cleansing. This is calculated according to the value of the house and is (the) responsibility of the owner of the property. If the house belongs to a residents' association, there will be an annual contribution which varies according to the type of association. On top (of this), of course, are the normal expenses, light, gas, telephone, etc.

Mr Jackson:	Good. I think we have all the information we need for now. We'll wait for the vendor's decision and in the meantime we'll prepare the documents and the deposit arrangements. I'll speak to (*lit.* with) our solicitor so that he (can) begin to plan the searches on the property. I hope that there will be no unexpected problems like, for example, the construction of a main road near the house. Now, you need the name of our solicitor, here it is (*lit.* it you have) and also that of the bank through which we'll make the payment.
Sra Robles:	Jolly good. I'll get in touch (*lit.* communicate) with your solicitor as soon as I know if the vendor has accepted your offer or not. But, before, if you have any query, please get in contact with our office.
Mr Jackson:	Many thanks.
Sra Robles:	Thank *you* (*lit.* to you) and goodbye, Mr and Mrs Jackson.
Mr Jackson:	Goodbye, señora Robles.

Checklist 10

Masculine nouns:

el recorrido	tour
el chalet	house
el dormitorio	bedroom
el garaje	garage
el aficionado	enthusiast, fan
el bricolaje	do-it-yourself
el tiempo	time
el millón	million
el atractivo	appeal, charm
los alrededores	setting, surroundings
el pino	pine tree
el niño	child, little boy
el dueño	owner
el número	number
el amigo	friend
el vendedor	vendor
el contrato	contract
el documento	document
el pasaporte	passport
el carnet de identidad	identity card
el notario	notary

el depósito	deposit
el préstamo	loan
el préstamo hipotecario	mortgage
el tipo de cambio	exchange rate
el crédito	loan
los fondos	funds
los daños	damages
los perjuicios	damages
el comprador	buyer
los trámites	transactions, arrangements
el abogado	solicitor, lawyer
el retraso	delay
el resto	rest, balance
los derechos	fees (professional)
el impuesto	tax
el IVA	VAT
el Ayuntamiento	town hall
el valor	value
el vecino	resident, neighbour
el gas	gas

Feminine nouns:

la residencia	residence
la zona	area, zone
la propiedad	property
la ubicación	location, position
la reforma	improvement, reform
la escala	range, scale
la peseta	peseta
la foto(grafía)	photo(graph)
las inmediaciones	surroundings
la urbanización	residential development
la vista	view
la sierra	mountain range
la piscina	swimming pool
la hora	time, hour
la dirección	address
la manera	way, manner
la compra	purchase
la opción	option
la cuenta	account
la indemnización	compensation
la vez	time
la obligación	obligation
la parte	party, side
la garantía	guarantee
la escritura	title deed(s)

la firma	signing, signature
las investigaciones	searches
la cuestión	matter
la contribución	tax (payment)
la limpieza	clean(s)ing
la responsabilidad	responsibility
la comunidad de vecinos	residents' association
la luz	light, electricity
la información	information
la decisión	decision
la construcción	construction
la autovía	main road
la duda	doubt, query

Verbs:

fijar residencia	to take up residence
comprar	to buy
importar	to matter
mirar	to look at
elegir	to choose (stem-changing e→i)
comunicar	to tell, pass on
dar a	to look out on, overlook
ofrecer	to offer (like conocer Checknote 28)
valer la pena	to be worthwhile
pagar	to pay
proponerse	to propose
financiar	to finance
hablar	to talk
transferir	to transfer (stem-changing e→i)
ocurrir	to happen
retirarse	to withdraw
reclamar	to claim
firmar	to sign
pasar	to happen
depender de	to depend on
concluir	to conclude (like disminuir)
oír decir	to hear (it said)
inscribir	to register, record
registrar	to register
cubrir	to cover
calcular	to calculate
pertenecer	to belong (like conocer)
variar	to vary (see Checknote 116)
esperar	to hope, wait for, expect
comunicarse	to be/get in touch
ponerse en contacto	to get in contact

Irregular verbs:

valer ('to be worth')
Present Tense: **valgo, vales, vale, valemos valéis, valen**
Future Tense: **valdré, valdrás,** etc.
Present Subjunctive: **valga, valgas,** etc.

venir ('to come')
Present Tense: **vengo, vienes, viene, venimos, venís, vienen**
Present Participle: **viniendo**
Future Tense: **vendré, vendrás,** etc.
Preterite Tense: **vine, viniste, vino, vinimos, vinisteis, vinieron**
Present Subjunctive: **venga, vengas,** etc.
Imperative: **ven (tú)**

Adjectives:

varios -as (f.)	several, a number of
adosado	semi-detached
de segunda mano	second-hand
habitable	(in)habitable
encantador -ora (f.)	charming
bonito	pretty, attractive
habitado	occupied
algún que otro	the odd ... or two (see Checknote 114)
necesario	necessary
estable	stable
convencido	convinced
arreglado	arranged, settled
cualquier -a (f.)	any
adicional	additional
absoluto	total, complete
normal	normal
intermedio	intermediary
aproximado	approximate
relacionado con	related to
municipal	local, municipal
inesperado	unexpected

Adverbs:

temprano	early
detenidamente	at great length, thoroughly
preferiblemente	preferably
tampoco	neither
más o menos	approximately
a lo mejor	probably, maybe
totalmente	totally
una vez	once
libremente	freely

Expressions:

un poco	a little, a bit
sobre todo	especially
he aquí	here is/are
querida	dear (*fem.*)
en casa	at home, in the house of
tener algo	to have (a certain) appeal/charm
es decir	that's to say
lo antes posible	as soon as possible
al contado	in cash, cash
dado	given, in view of
en teoría	in theory
por nuestra cuenta	on our own account, independently
como mucho	at most
en comparación con	in comparison to
entonces	then
del orden de	in the order of
por ejemplo	for example
encima	on top
entretanto	meantime

Conjunctions:

para que	in order/so that
una vez que	once
en cuanto a	as soon as

Prepositions:

detrás	behind
ante	before, in the presence of
a través de	through

CHECKNOTES

107 Imperative with **tú**

Clearly Mr and Mrs Jackson will use the familiar form of 'you' when talking to each other. In Unit 7 (Checknote 71) you learnt how to make affirmative polite commands (**Vd.** and **Vds.**) and negative polite and familiar commands using the subjunctive. Now we want to show you how to tell someone who you know well what to do, i.e. using the imperative with **tú**. It is formed like this:

Regular verbs:

hablar → **habla**	speak! (*sing. fam.*)
correr → **corre**	run! (*sing. fam.*)
escribir→ **escribe**	write! (*sing. fam.*)

Stem-changing verbs:

probar → **prueba**	try! (*sing. fam.*)
volver → **vuelve**	come back! (*sing. fam.*)
pedir → **pide**	ask! (*sing. fam.*)

Some Irregulars:

decir → **di**	tell! (*sing. fam.*)
venir → **ven**	come! (*sing. fam.*)
hacer → **haz**	do! (*sing. fam.*)
poner → **pon**	put! (*sing. fam.*)
tener → **ten**	have! (*sing. fam.*)

Remember, any pronouns are tagged on to the <u>end</u> of the imperative (and an accent may have to be added to maintain the original pronunciation), for example:

Háblame.	Speak to me.
Escríbela.	Write it.
Pídeselo.	Ask him for it.
Escúchame.	Listen to me.
Dile que no.	Tell him no.
Siéntate.	Sit down.
Ponlo en la mesa.	Put it on the table.

Don't forget … <u>all the negative</u> commands use the subjunctive:

No cierres la puerta.
Don't close the door.

No vacile en llamarnos, señor.
Don't hesitate to call us, sir.

No me esperes.
Don't wait for me.

108 Some more numbers

In Checknote 90, we introduced the numbers up to and including the thousands. However, when it comes to house/car prices and salaries, you'll need to be thinking in millions of pesetas.

Here's how to express such figures:

un millón	1,000,000
dos millones	2,000,000

Millón is a masculine noun and is used like this:

un millón de pesetas   a million pesetas

cincuenta y tres millones de habitantes
53 million inhabitants

Cuesta tres millones, cuatrocientas doce mil, novecientas treinta y cinco pesetas.
It costs 3,412,935 pesetas!

You'll have already noticed that when English uses a comma in figures, Spanish uses a full stop:

2.000	**dos mil**
2,000	**two thousand**

109 Percentages

In Spanish an article precedes the percentage, like this:

El 40 por ciento prefiere la cerveza alemana.
40 per cent prefer German beer.

Sólo un 6 por ciento considera que la situación ha mejorado.
Only (a) 6 per cent consider that the situation has improved.

110 Irregular verbs in the preterite tense

A group of verbs is formed from irregular 'stems' in the preterite tense. The 'stems' differ, but there is one set of endings common to them all.

Tener ('to have') and **poner** ('to put') belong to this group:

tuve	I had	puse	I put
tuviste	you had	pusiste	you put
tuvo	he/she/you had	puso	he/she/you put
tuvimos	we had	pusimos	we put
tuvisteis	you had	pusisteis	you put
tuvieron	they/you had	pusieron	they/you put

Examples:

Tuve una entrevista con los directores.
I had an interview with the directors.

Tuvimos que volver.
We had to go back.

Puso los documentos en la mesa.
He put the documents on the table.

Se pusieron en contacto con el agente.
They got in touch with the agent.

Hacer ('to do, make') also belongs in this group. You will have noticed **hicimos** ('we did') in the dialogue. Here is the rest of the tense. Notice the '**z**' spelling in **hizo** in order to retain the **th** sound:

hice	I did, made
hiciste	you did, made
hizo	he/she/you did, made
hicimos	we did, made
hiciste	you did, made
hicieron	they/you did, made

Example:

Hizo el trabajo y luego salió.
He did the work and then left.

No hice nada el fin de semana.
I didn't do anything at the weekend.

Some other irregular verbs of this type:

venir → vine	('I came')
poder → pude	('I could')
estar → estuve	('I was')

Vinieron en tren.
They came by train.

No pude hacerlo.
I couldn't do it.

Estuvimos en Barcelona ayer.
We were in Barcelona yesterday.

111 Spelling changes in the preterite

In Checknote 96 you learnt that in order to maintain the original pronunciation of verbs ending in **-ZAR**, a spelling change occurs in the first person singular, like this:

empezar ('to begin') → **empecé, empezaste, empezó,** etc.

A spelling change also occurs for the same reason in verbs ending in **-GAR** and **-CAR**:

pagar ('to pay') → **pagué, pagaste, pagó,** etc.
llegar ('to arrive') → **llegué, llegaste, llegó,** etc.
convocar ('to call') → **convoqué, convocaste, convocó,** etc.

Examples:

Yo pagué la cuenta.
I paid the bill.

Convoqué la reunión para mañana.
I called the meeting for tomorrow.

112 Preterite tense of stem-changing -IR verbs

Stem-changing **-IR** verbs are irregular in the 3rd persons of the preterite tense, for example:

elegir 'to choose'		**sentir** 'to feel'	
elegí	I chose	**sentí**	I felt
elegiste	you chose	**sentiste**	you felt
eligió	he/she/you chose	**sintió**	he/she/you felt
elegimos	we chose	**sentimos**	we felt
elegisteis	you chose	**sentisteis**	you felt
eligieron	they/you chose	**sintieron**	they/you felt

Some examples:

Eligieron el chalet con el jardín.
They chose the house with the garden.

El camarero nos sirvió rápidamente.
The waiter served us quickly.

113 Further uses of the subjunctive

a) Conjunctions

i) In Unit 7 (Checknote 70) we introduced you to two conjunctions which are normally followed by the subjunctive. Here is one more:

para que   in order to, so that

For example:

Os mandan más detalles sobre las propiedades para que podáis llegar a una decisión.
They're sending you more details on the properties in order that you can reach a decision.

ii) Expressions of time

Some expressions of time such as **en cuanto** ('as soon as') and **una vez que** ('once') are followed by the subjunctive only when the action has not yet taken place.

Study the following:

Te llamó en cuanto llegó a casa.
She called you immediately she got home.

BUT

Te llamará en cuanto llegue a casa.
She'll call you immediately she gets home.

Pudieron pagar el depósito una vez que recibieron los fondos necesarios de Inglaterra.
They could/managed to pay the deposit once they received the necessary funds from England.

BUT

Llámame una vez que hayas hablado con tu mujer.
Call me once you've talked with your wife.

In the first sentence of each pair, the subjunctive is not needed because the action is a reality or has happened.

Some more examples:

Les mandará la carta en cuanto haya recibido la información.
He'll send them the letter as soon as he has received the information.

Os escribirá una vez que tenga todos los detalles.
He'll write to you once he has all the details.

b) **Puede que** ('may')

The subjunctive is also used after expressions of possibility like
puede que ... = ... may ...

Examples:

Va a Venezuela.
He's going to Venezuela.

BUT

Puede que vaya a Venezuela.
He may be going to Venezuela.

Ya ha salido.
He has already left.

BUT

Puede que ya haya salido.
He may have already left.

Puede que tenga que volver a Inglaterra.
He may have to return to England.

Puede que haga más frío mañana.
It may be colder tomorrow.

c) Expressions of uncertainty

In Unit 7 you learnt that verbs expressing uncertainty are followed
by the subjunctive. When a verb of confirmation, certainty, or
observation becomes negative, an element of doubt or uncertainty
is expressed, and therefore the verb in the dependent clause will
take the subjunctive. Here are some examples:

Nos dieron la garantía de que iban a aceptar nuestra oferta.
They gave us the guarantee that they were going to accept our offer.

BUT

No tenemos ninguna garantía de que vayan a aceptar nuestra oferta.
We have no guarantee that they are going to accept our offer.

Estoy convencido de que tienes razón.
I am convinced you are right.

BUT

No estoy convencido de que vayan a llegar a tiempo.
I'm not convinced they are going to arrive on time.

No hay garantía de que hayan recibido tu carta.
There's no guarantee that they have received your letter.

No estamos convencidos de que estos ordenadores sean los mejores.
We are not convinced that these PCs are the best.

d) **Rogar que** ... ('to request that')

This is a formal expression, requiring the use of the subjunctive, and can be translated as 'Kindly ...', like this:

Le ruego que me mande la carta lo antes posible.
Kindly (*lit.* I request you to) send me the letter as soon as possible.

Sometimes the **que** can be omitted:

Se ruega no fumen en la sala de conferencias.
Kindly do not smoke in the conference hall (*lit.* it is requested you do not smoke ...).

114 **Algún que otro** ... ('the odd ... or two')
     Alguna que otra ...

This phrase agrees in gender with the noun it precedes, for example:

Hizo algún que otro viaje a España.
He made the odd trip or two to Spain.

Puede que ocurra alguna que otra dificultad.
A few odd difficulties may occur.

¿Has tenido problemas? – Sí, alguno que otro.
Have you had (any) problems? – Yes, the odd one or two.

115 **El IVA (Impuesto sobre el Valor Añadido)** ('VAT')

VAT regulations in Spain are not quite the same as in England and the amount payable on different types of goods varies.

116 Verbs ending in -IAR

In some verbs ending in -**IAR**, the 'i' is stressed, and therefore in the present tense and subjunctive an accent is written. For example:

enviar ('to send')

Present Tense: **envío, envías, envía, enviamos, enviáis, envían**
Subjunctive: **envíe, envíes, envíe, enviemos, enviéis, envíen**

Example:

Su abuela le envía solamente una tarjeta.
Her grandmother sends her only a card.

Other verbs of this type are:

variar ('to vary')
ampliar ('to extend, expand')

For example:

Las condiciones varían según el cliente.
The terms vary according to the customer.

Puede que amplíen la fábrica en los próximos años.
They may expand the factory in the next few years.

117 Debería ('should, ought')

In Unit 4 (Checknote 38) we introduced you to the verb **deber** ('must'), for example:

Debo terminar el trabajo.
I must finish the work.

When **deber** is used in the conditional tense it means 'should' or 'ought', like this:

Debería informarles inmediatamente.
He ought to inform them immediately.

No deberías hacer esto.
You shouldn't do that.

Deberíamos ponernos en contacto con el director.
We ought to get in touch with the director.

Comprehension Practice 10

Look at the conversation at the beginning of the unit and answer these questions:

1 ¿Cuál es la primera pregunta importante que hace la señora Robles a los señores Jackson?
2 ¿Qué hicieron los señores Jackson la semana pasada?
3 ¿Cómo es la casa que busca la señora Jackson?
4 ¿Por qué no quiere hacer reformas el señor Jackson?
5 ¿Cuál es el precio que están dispuestos a pagar?
6 De los tres chalets que ven, ¿cuál prefieren?
7 ¿Van a pedir un préstamo hipotecario?
8 ¿Qué tienen que incluir con el contrato de compraventa?
9 ¿Qué ocurrirá si los señores Jackson deciden retirarse de la compra una vez firmado el contrato de compraventa?
10 ¿Tendrán que pagar el precio total cuando firmen el contrato de compraventa?
11 ¿Qué gastos intermedios hay?
12 ¿Cuánto es el IVA que se paga sobre una propiedad de segunda mano?
13 ¿Qué gastos hay que pagar como dueño de una propiedad?
14 ¿Pagan la misma contribución al Ayuntamiento todos los dueños?
15 Mientras esperan la decisión del vendedor, ¿qué van a hacer los señores Jackson?
16 ¿Qué tipo de problema inesperado podría surgir según el señor Jackson?
17 ¿Con quién se comunicará la señora Robles una vez que sepa si el vendedor acepta la oferta o no?

FLUENCY PRACTICE 54

Some new words you'll need for the following practice:

el verano	summer
el invierno	winter
Tailandia	Thailand
el Canadá	Canada
anoche	last night
esta mañana	this morning

Chatting with a colleague, you find yourself in the position of having pre-empted most of his intentions or plans! Look at the example, and using the cues provided make up similar responses. You'll need to use the preterite tense. (Perhaps a look back at Checknotes 93 and 104 will help too.)

Colleague: **Este verano vamos a Tailandia.**
This summer we're going to Thailand.

Cue: wife and I/there/last year

You: **Mi mujer y yo fuimos allí el año pasado.**
My wife and I went there last year.

1 Vamos a terminar el trabajo esta tarde.
[I/mine/yesterday.]
2 Van a hacer las investigaciones mañana.
[we/ours/last Friday]
3 Este invierno pensamos ir al Canadá.
[my children/there/last winter]
4 Escribiré mi carta después de comer.
[María/hers/last night]
5 Vamos a comprar un apartamento en Marbella.
[Mr and Mrs Smith/one there/two years ago]
6 Nos pondremos en contacto con los agentes el lunes.
[I/with them/last week]
7 Tendremos que cambiar dinero mañana.
[I/£260/this morning]

FLUENCY PRACTICE 55

New words:

la cena	dinner, supper, evening meal
la fiesta	party
el marido	husband

Subjunctive or not?

In each of the following sentences change if necessary the verb in brackets to the correct form:

1 Queremos (**comprar**) un chalet.
2 Busca un puesto que (**pagar**) bien.
3 Siento que tu mujer no (**poder**) venir a la cena.
4 Creo que su jefe (**tener**) razón.
5 En cuanto (**llegar**), llamó a su mujer.

6 Póngase en contacto con nosotros una vez que (**haber**) llegado a una decisión.

7 Me alegro de que (**ir**) a la fiesta con tu marido.

FLUENCY PRACTICE 56

New words:

la cocina	kitchen
amueblado	fitted, furnished
el baño	bath(room)
el salón	sitting-room
el dinero	money
la chimenea	fire (place), chimney
los trámites	procedures
la calefacción	heating
la zona común	communal area
ponerse de acuerdo	to come to an agreement
componerse de	to consist of (like **poner**), to be made up of
tomar una decisión	to make a decision
heredar	to inherit

Study again the conversation at the beginning of this unit and then take the part of Mr Brown in the following dialogue with a Spanish estate agent:

Mr Brown: Good morning. I would like some additional information on a house in the Galapagar residential development.

Sra Robles: ¡Cómo no! Siéntese por favor. ¿Cuál es el chalet que le interesa más?

Mr Brown: The semi-detached one, with three bedrooms, which looks out on to the mountain range. How much is it?

Sra Robles: Vale 32 millones de pesetas. Tiene dos baños, cocina amueblada, salón amplio con chimenea, calefacción ...

Mr Brown: What facilities does the development have?

Sra Robles: Dispone de zonas comunes, piscina y tenis, garaje ...

Mr Brown: Is the house occupied?

Sra Robles: No, no. Es de construcción nueva.

Mr Brown: Is it possible to go and see it today?

Sra Robles: Claro que sí.

Later that day . . .

Mr Brown: I like the house a lot. Once one makes the offer, what are the normal procedures?

Sra Robles: Comunicamos su oferta al vendedor. Si la acepta, le mandamos un contrato de compraventa.

Mr Brown: A Sale Contract? What's that exactly?

Sra Robles: Es un acuerdo firmado entre las dos partes, o sea el comprador y el vendedor. ¿Cómo va a financiar la compra?

Mr Brown: With money I've inherited from my grandparents.

Sra Robles: ¿Así que no va a pedir un préstamo hipotecario?

Mr Brown: No. The funds have already been transferred from England. Do I have to make an initial payment?

Sra Robles: Sí. Debe pagar un depósito inicial de un 10 por ciento.

Mr Brown: And when does one pay the rest?

Sra Robles: Cuando se firme la Escritura.

Mr Brown: How long should one reckon between the signing of the contract and that of the Deeds?

Sra Robles: Puede ser cuestión de unos días o más. Vd. y el vendedor se ponen de acuerdo sobre la fecha cuando se firme el Contrato.

Mr Brown: What happens if I withdraw from the purchase?

Sra Robles: Pierde el depósito.

Mr Brown: Over and above the price of the house, what costs are there?

Sra Robles: Los gastos se componen de los derechos del notario, los costes de inscribir la propiedad, y el IVA al 6 por ciento del precio.

Mr Brown: Okay. I think I have all the information I need for now. I'll have to talk with my wife before making an offer. She may have very different ideas. When we've made a decision, I'll get in touch with you.

DICTIONARY PRACTICE 3˙

Look at the following advertisements from an estate agency newspaper, and then answer the questions which follow:

PROPIEDADES EXCLUSIVAS GARCÍA S.L.

C/PASTORES 4, 3a planta
(Metro Guzmán el Bueno)

LE OFRECE:

Juan Manuel García
Agente de la Propiedad Inmobiliaria 123
Miembro de FIABCI (España)

PISOS EN VENTA

Vaguada: 120 m^2, 3 dormitorios, baño y aseo, 2 salones, 2 terrazas, calefacción central, gas ciudad, exterior, reformar.

Moncloa: 80 m^2, 2 dormitorios, baño, exterior, cocina amueblada, calefacción individual por gas, ascensor, portero, excelente conservación, luminoso, inmejorable.

Delicias: 100 m^2, 3 dormitorios, 2 baños y aseo, buena conservación, calefacción central, garaje, suelos de parquet, piscina, terraza, mucha luz, precioso.

Salamanca: 85 m^2, 3 dormitorios, baño, salón-comedor, mucha luz, necesita reforma. OCASIÓN ¡¡16.000.000!!

P. de Extremadura: dúplex, 135 + 80 de terraza, 3 dormitorios, 2 baños, salón-comedor, totalmente nuevo, con mucha luz, precioso.

C.Caminos: 140 m^2, 2 dormitorios, 2 baños, ascensor, exterior, a estrenar.

CHALETS

Las Lomas Bosque: Vacío, lujo, 4 dormitorios, 4 baños, salón con chimenea, comedor de 80 m^2, 2 trasteros, garaje, jardín, piscina.

La Moraleja: Vivienda adosada, 3 dormitorios, salón, comedor, cocina, vestíbulo, dos baños, aseo, despacho, garaje. 13.900.000 ptas.

Vila Franca Castillo: 220 m^2, 500 de parcela, 5 dormitorios, 3 baños, aseo, cocina-office, salón amplio con chimenea francesa, garaje, trastero, etc. Total: 19.850.000.

Alcobendas: 200 m^2, 4 dormitorios, 2 baños, aseo, buhardilla, bodega, garaje 4 coches, piscina, a negociar.

¿DESEA VENDER O COMPRAR?
LA GESTIÓN DEL AGENTE DE LA PROPIEDAD INMOBILIARIA
LE AHORRARÍA TIEMPO Y MOLESTIAS. LLÁMENOS. TEL 512-34-56

Which advertisements would attract your attention if …

1 you do quite a lot of work at home for which you need peace and quiet?
2 you're looking for a bargain?
3 you and your wife are looking for a smart, bright little place, ready to move in, with service and lift?
4 the family and the dogs will need space?
5 you like quiet weekends out of town round the pool; you also need somewhere to put the boat and trailer which the kids use during the holidays?
6 you want a house you can move into immediately?

Which ads would you immediately cross off your list if …

7 you want a detached house?
8 you hate DIY and are hopeless at it?

S E R V I C I O S
I N M O B I L I A R I O S

*In addition to banks, there is a large network of **CAJAS** throughout Spain. These are savings banks, which also provide many of the services offered by British building societies.*

Promoting products in Mexico

In this unit we introduce you to some of the differences which exist between Spanish as spoken in Spain (Peninsular Spanish) and the Spanish spoken in Mexico. Some useful vocabulary about trade fairs is included, as is a new past tense, the imperfect.

Mr Jackson is now well settled in his new job in Spain. One of his projects is to promote the company's products in Mexico. Part of the campaign will be to take a stand at the High-tech fair in Mexico City. Here he is discussing the details of exhibiting at the fair with his Mexican colleague, Guillermo Elizondo. Since they know each other well, naturally they use tú, the familiar form of 'you'.

Sr Elizondo: ... total que el Consejo ha aceptado tu propuesta de participar en la Feria INTERTEC de México.

Mr Jackson: Sí, tal como yo esperaba, les parecía una ocasión ideal para promover nuestra nueva gama de equipos, especialmente el ordenador portátil plegable y el 'notebook'. La mayoría de nuestros competidores estarán representados allí y nuestra presencia es imprescindible si queremos penetrar en el mercado latinoamericano. ¿Cuáles son las fechas exactas de la exposición?

Sr Elizondo: Tendrá lugar del 9 al 15 de febrero, así es que cuanto antes empecemos a organizarnos, mejor.

Mr Jackson: De acuerdo. Bueno, Guillermo, cuento con tu experiencia en esto. Sé que el año pasado organizaste la representación de una compañía en este mismo recinto en México, y según tengo entendido, fue un gran éxito.

Sr Elizondo: Gracias. Bien, primero tenemos que reservar el stand. Trataré de conseguir que nos ubiquen en un buen sitio. Queremos llamar la atención y no pasar inadvertidos en un rincón. Los stands normales disponen de una superficie de doce metros cuadrados. Podemos pedir más espacio si esto te parece poco.

Mr Jackson: Vamos a ver. No sólo nos hace falta espacio para instalar las máquinas, sino que también nos convendría tener un sitio donde los visitantes puedan probar los equipos, y una sala donde se pueda hablar tranquilamente con los clientes.

Sr Elizondo: De acuerdo. Además tenemos que presentar nuestro material publicitario. El departamento de Mercadotecnia ya está preparando unos diseños, te los podemos enseñar luego.

Mr Jackson: Bien. Y en cuanto al pago del stand. ¿Cuáles son los trámites?

Sr Elizondo: Normalmente se paga un depósito, un 12 ó 15 por ciento del importe total, en el momento de hacer la reservación, y el resto después de que se haya confirmado la reservación.

Mr Jackson: Entonces habla con Enrique en Finanzas y asegúrate de que él conoce todos los detalles.

Sr Elizondo: Sí, sí, no te preocupes. Luego hablaré con él. ¿A cuántas personas vamos a mandar? Necesitaremos representantes en el stand todo el día, y unos técnicos para la instalación de los equipos.

Mr Jackson: Hasta ahora no he pensado en quiénes, además de nosostros. De todos modos, no creo que tengamos muchos problemas en conseguir un equipo. Aunque trabajar en una feria puede ser duro, la oportunidad de pasar una semana en México, bueno, ¡no es de despreciar!

Sr Elizondo: ¡Tienes razón! En cuanto hayas formado el equipo, dímelo, porque tendré que organizar el alojamiento y los pases a la exposición. También me encargaré de transportar el equipo del aeropuerto a la feria, y creo que los organizadores disponen de apoyo técnico dentro de la exposición.

Mr Jackson: Otra cuestión a tener en cuenta es la seguridad.

Sr Elizondo: En cuanto al traslado de los equipos, los costos caen a cuenta nuestra. Recuerdo que el año pasado siempre había un alto nivel de seguridad y un sistema de control de entrada muy eficaz.

Mr Jackson: Bien. ¿Y qué otras instalaciones había?

Sr Elizondo: Las instalaciones eran realmente estupendas. En el salón se contaba con todo – servicio de traductores, salas de reuniones y conferencias, algunas con telex y fax, restaurantes y bares.

Mr Jackson: Perfecto. ¡Sólo nos falta tener éxito en la venta de nuestros productos!

Sr Elizondo: Bueno, Peter, déjame poner estos detalles en marcha. Es todavía demasiado temprano para llamar a México – lo haré esta tarde y te pondré al día con respecto al stand tan pronto como reciba contestación.

Mr Jackson: Vale. No dejes de mantenerme al corriente, Guillermo. Y gracias.

Sr Elizondo: De nada.

TRANSLATION

Sr Elizondo: . . . so, the board has accepted your proposal to participate in the Intertec Trade Fair in Mexico.

Mr Jackson: Yes, just as I was expecting, it seemed to them the ideal opportunity to promote our new range of equipment, especially the lap-top (lit. PC portable foldable) and the notebook. The majority of our competitors will be (represented) there and our presence is vital if we want to get into the Latin-American market. What are the exact dates of the exhibition?

Sr Elizondo: It will take place from 9th to 15th February, so the sooner we start to get organized, the better.

Mr Jackson: I agree. Well, Guillermo, I'm relying on your experience in this. I know that last year you organized the representation of a company in this same place in Mexico, and, as I understand, it was a great success.

Sr Elizondo: Thank you. Well, first we have to book the stand. I'll try to get them to locate us (lit. that they locate us) in a good spot. We want to attract (lit. call) attention and not go unnoticed in a corner. The normal stands are (lit. have an area of) 12 square metres. We can ask for more space if you think this is not enough (*lit.* this to you seems little).

Mr Jackson: Let's see. We need space not only for the installation of the machines, but also it would be as well for us (*lit.* it would suit us) to have a place where visitors can try out the machines and a room where one can talk undisturbed with customers.

Sr Elizondo: I agree. In addition we have to display our advertising material. The Marketing Department is already preparing some designs, we can show you them later.

Mr Jackson: Fine. As regards the payment of the stand. What are the arrangements?

Sr Elizondo: Normally you pay a deposit, 12 or 15 per cent of the total amount, when you make (*lit.* at the moment of making) the booking, and the balance after the booking has been confirmed.

Mr Jackson: Then have a word (*lit.* speak) with Enrique in Finance (Department) and make sure that he knows all the details.

Sr Elizondo: Yes, yes, don't worry. I'll speak to him later. How many people are we going to send? We'll need reps on the stand all day, and some technicians for setting up the machines.

Mr Jackson: Up to now I haven't thought about who, apart from us. At any rate, I don't think we'll have much problem (*lit.* many problems) in getting (together) a team. Although working at a fair can be tough, the chance of spending a week in Mexico, well, it's not one to be sniffed at!

Sr Elizondo: You're right! As soon as you have got (*lit.* formed) the team, let me know (*lit.* tell me it), because I will have to arrange accommodation and exhibition passes. I'll also deal with transporting the equipment from the airport to the fair, and I believe that the organizers have technical assistance available within the exhibition.

Mr Jackson: Another thing (*lit.* matter) to bear in mind is the security.

Sr Elizondo: As regards the equipment in transit (*lit.* the transfer of the equipment), the costs are our responsibility (*lit.* fall to our account). I remember that last year there was always a high level of security and a very efficient entry control system.

Mr Jackson: Fine. And what other facilities were there?

Sr Elizondo: The facilities were really great. In the exhibition hall, they (*lit.* one) had everything – a translation (*lit.* translators')

service, conference and lecture rooms/theatres, some
with telex and fax, restaurants and bars.

Mr Jackson: Perfect! All we need now is (*lit.* Only we need) to be
successful in selling (*lit.* the sale of) our products!

Sr Elizondo: Right then, Peter. Leave me to get going on these details
(*lit.* to put these details into motion). It's still too early to
phone Mexico – I'll do that (*lit.* it) this afternoon, and I'll let
you know about the stand as soon as I get (a) reply.

Mr Jackson: Okay. Please (*lit.* don't fail to) keep me posted, Guillermo!
And thanks.

Sr Elizondo: Not at all.

Checklist 11

Masculine nouns:

el Consejo	board, council
el competidor	competitor
el recinto	place, enclosure
el stand	stand
el sitio	spot, place
el rincón	corner
el metro	metre
el espacio	space
el visitante	visitor
el aeropuerto	airport
el organizador	organizer
el apoyo	assistance, support, help
el alojamiento	accommodation
el pase	pass
el traslado	transfer
el costo*	cost
el control	control
el salón	(exhibition) hall, rooms
el traductor	translator

Feminine nouns:

la propuesta	proposal
la ocasión	opportunity
la exposición	exhibition
la atención	attention
la superficie	area, surface
la sala	hall, room
la mercadotecnia*	marketing

la reservación*	booking, reservation
las finanzas	finances
la persona	person
la seguridad	security
la entrada	entrance
la conferencia	lecture, conference
la contestación	reply

Verbs:

promover	to promote (stem-changing o → ue)
estar representado	to be represented
tener lugar	to take place
organizarse	to get organized
ubicar	to locate
hacer falta	to be wanting, necessary (see Checknote 123)
instalar	to install, set up
convenir	to suit, be good/suitable for (like venir, see Unit 10)
asegurarse de	to make sure of
preocuparse	to be/get worried/concerned
encargarse de	to be in/take charge of
transportar	to transport
despreciar	to sniff at, scorn
formar	to form
caer	to fall (like traer)
recordar	to remember (stem-changing o → ue)
faltar	to be missing, lacking (see Checknote 123)
dejar	to leave, let
poner en marcha	to set in motion, get going
mantener al corriente	to keep informed, posted, up-to-date

Adjectives:

ideal	ideal
portátil	portable
plegable	foldable
imprescindible	vital, essential
latinoamericano	Latin-American
inadvertido	unnoticed
cuadrado	square
total	total
duro	hard, tough

Adverbs:

| sólo | only |
| tranquilamente | undisturbed, uninterrupted, peacefully |

luego	later on
realmente	really
todavía	still

Preposition:

| además de | besides |

Conjunctions:

después de que	after (see Checknote 120a)
aunque	although
tan pronto como	as soon as (see Checknote 120a)

Expressions:

total que	and so, so, to cut a long story short ...
tal como	just as
cuanto antes ...	the sooner ... (see Checknote 120b)
llamar la atención	to attract attention
pasar inadvertido	to go unnoticed
vamos a ver	let's see
de todos modos	anyway, at any rate
en efecto	in fact
con respecto a	with regard to
vale	okay, fine
no dejes de ...	don't fail to ... (*fam.*)
de nada	not at all

*See Checknote 118

CHECKNOTES

118 Mexican versus Peninsular Spanish

a) Pronunciation

You'll have noticed that Guillermo Elizondo's pronunciation is different from that of Peter Jackson. There are many variations of Spanish pronunciation within South and Central America and within Mexico itself there exist regional differences. Here are some of the more common aspects:

Mexicans tend to speak more slowly and softly than Spaniards and pronounce the consonants more clearly.

They do not use the lisping 'th' sound for 'z' or 'c' before 'e' and 'i'. They pronounce these as an 's' (as in the English 'missing'). For example, cinco is pronounced séen-koh, Martínez, Mahrr-tée-ness.

'll' is pronounced as a 'y' but can veer more towards an English 'j' in Mexico, as in llama yáh-mah or ella áy-jah.

's' at the end of a word is often slightly aspirated or omitted, as in los dos – loh doh, but otherwise it is more forcefully pronounced than in Peninsular Spanish.

'j' is pronounced almost like 'h' as in 'hand'.

'x' has a variety of pronunciations particularly in names of places in Mexico. It's probably best if you learn each one as you come across it.

b) Vocabulary

Some words which occur in Peninsular Spanish have variations or alternatives which are more commonly used in Mexican Spanish. For example reservación instead of reserva, costo instead of coste, mercadotecnia is often rendered by the anglicism márketing in Peninsular Spanish. These words are marked with an asterisk in the Checklists.

c) México versus Méjico

Both spellings exist. In Spain the 'j' spelling is strictly speaking the correct spelling, although many of the Spanish newspapers are now using the 'x' spelling. In Mexico, however, the 'x' spelling only is the correct one.

In either case the pronunciation reflects the 'j' spelling (Máy-Hee-koh in Spain and Máy-hee-koh in Mexico).

Similarly, mexicano and mejicano ('Mexican') both exist.

119 Imperfect tense

You already know how to talk in the past in Spanish, using the perfect and preterite tenses:

Hemos vendido la casa.	We have sold the house.
Escribí la carta.	I wrote the letter.
¿Fuiste a Madrid?	Did you go to Madrid?

There's another tense, the imperfect, which is used when we want to express what we were doing or used to do, or to describe something with reference to the past, as opposed to a completed event in the past:

Trabajaba en el stand cuando llegó el primer cliente.
I was working on the stand when the first customer arrived.

Vivía en Londres.
I used to live in London.

El chalet estaba situado cerca del aeropuerto.
The house was situated near the airport.

To form the imperfect tense, take the 'stem' of the verb and add the following endings:

a) **-AR** verbs:

comprar ('to buy')

compr**aba**	I used to buy, was buying
compr**abas**	you used to buy, were buying
compr**aba**	he/she/it used to buy, etc.
	you used to buy, etc.
compr**ábamos**	we used to buy, etc.
compr**abais**	you used to buy, etc.
compr**aban**	they used to buy, etc.
	you used to buy, etc.

b) **-ER** and **-IR** verbs:

vender ('to sell')

vend**ía**	I used to sell
vend**ías**	you used to sell
vend**ía**	he/she/it used to sell
	you used to sell
vend**íamos**	we used to sell
vend**íais**	you used to sell
vend**ían**	they used to sell
	you used to sell

vivir ('to live')

viv**ía**	I used to live
viv**ías**	you used to live
viv**ía**	he/she/it used to live
	you used to live
viv**íamos**	we used to live
viv**íais**	you used to live
viv**ían**	they used to live
	you used to live

Examples:

Juan siempre salía de la oficina a las cinco.
John always used to leave/left the office at five.

Exportábamos mucho a Europa.
We used to export a lot to Europe.

El stand estaba ubicado en un rincón.
The stand was located in a corner.

Tenías razón.
You were right.

Había mucha gente en el aeropuerto.
There were lots of people in the airport.

There are only three irregular verbs in the imperfect:

ir 'to go'

iba	I used to go, was going
ibas	you used to go, etc.
iba	he/she/it used to go, etc.
	you used to go, etc.
íbamos	we used to go, etc.
ibais	you used to go, etc.
iban	they used to go, etc.
	you used to go, etc.

ser 'to be'

era	I was
eras	you were
era	he/she/it was
	you were
éramos	we were
erais	you were
eran	they were
	you were

ver 'to see'

veía	I used to see
veías	you used to see
veía	he/she/it used to see
	you used to see
veíamos	we used to see
veíais	you used to see
veían	they used to see
	you used to see

Examples:

Íbamos al banco cuando vimos a Enrique.
We were going to the bank when we saw Henry.

Cuando yo era pequeño, iba a visitar a mis abuelos todos los domingos.
When I was small, I used to go and visit my grandparents every Sunday.

El señor González era el director.
Mr González was the director.

Veía a unos clientes y no podía salir.
He was seeing some customers and couldn't leave.

120 Further uses of the subjunctive

a) In Unit 10 you learnt that some expressions of time are followed by the subjunctive, when the action has not yet taken place. Here are two others:

después de que after
tan pronto como as soon as

Examples:

Decidiremos qué hacer después de que nuestros colegas hayan hablado con el director.
We'll decide what to do after our colleagues have spoken to the director.

BUT . . .

Convocaron una huelga después de que sus colegas hablaron con el director.
They called a strike after their colleagues spoke to the director.

Tan pronto como vuelva de su viaje, hablaré con él.
As soon as he returns from his trip, I'll speak to him.

BUT . . .

Tan pronto como volvió de su viaje, hablé con él.
As soon as he returned from his trip I spoke to him.

b) **Cuanto antes . . . mejor** The sooner . . . the better

Again, in this expression, since the event has not taken place, the verb requires the subjunctive, for example:

Cuanto antes escribamos la carta, mejor.
The sooner we write the letter, the better.

Cuanto antes compren un coche, mejor.
The sooner they buy a car, the better.

c) **Conseguir** ('to get, manage')

In Unit 7 (Checknotes 68 and 69) you learnt that some verbs require the subjunctive in a dependent clause introduced by **que**. **Conseguir** also follows this rule. For example:

> **Quiero conseguir un puesto en Barcelona.**
> I want to get a job in Barcelona.

> **No consigo hacerlo.**
> I can't manage to do it.

BUT

> **Siempre consigue que le manden un cheque cada mes.**
> He always gets them to send him a cheque every month.

> **Intentaré conseguir que nos esperen en la entrada.**
> I'll try to get them to wait for us at the entrance.

d) ... **una sala donde se pueda ...**

Look back at Unit 8 (Checknote 86). You'll remember that the subjunctive is used in sentences where the antecedent is not yet known. Such is the case here:

> **Queremos un sitio donde se pueda hablar tranquilamente.**
> We want a place where one can talk undisturbed.

> **Nos conviene tener un stand que disponga de una superficie de 20 metros cuadrados.**
> We could do with having a stand which has an area of 20 square metres.

121 Ó ('or')

O takes an accent when it appears between two numbers so as to avoid confusion with nought:

6 ó 7   6 or 7

BUT

seis o siete   six or seven

122 Personal pronouns with prepositions

Spanish uses the following pronouns after prepositions:

para <u>mí</u>	for <u>me</u>
además de <u>ti</u>	besides <u>you</u>
con <u>él</u>	with <u>him, it</u> (*masc.* thing)

de <u>ella</u>	about <u>her, it</u> (*fem.* thing)
después de <u>usted</u>	after <u>you</u>
para <u>sí</u>	for <u>himself/herself/yourself</u>
además de <u>nosotros</u>	besides <u>us</u>
para <u>vosotros</u>	for <u>you</u>
entre <u>ellos</u>	amongst <u>them</u> (*masc.*)
con <u>ellas</u>	with <u>them</u> (*fem.*)
por <u>ustedes</u>	on behalf of <u>you</u>

Examples:

Una cerveza para mí, ¿y para ti?
A beer for me, and for you?

Llegó después de nosotros.
He arrived after us.

With the preposition **con**, 'with', the forms **mí**, **ti** and **sí** become **conmigo**, **contigo** and **consigo**.

¿Vuelves conmigo?
Are you coming back with me?

¿Trabaja contigo?
Does he work with you?

Llevaba los documentos consigo.
She was carrying the documents with her (self).

123 Hacer falta ('to be necessary, wanting, to need')

This verb has a similar construction to gustar (see Checknote 77) in that the object of the verb in English becomes the subject in Spanish, like this:

Me hace falta más tiempo.
I need more time (*lit.* more time is necessary to me).

Nos hacen falta unos especialistas.
We need some specialists (*lit.* some specialists are necessary to us).

Hacía falta cambiarlo.
It needed changing.

Other verbs with this construction are:

faltar ('to be lacking/missing, to need')

Me faltaba dinero.
I needed/lacked money (*lit.* money was lacking to me).

Faltan muchos detalles.
Many details are missing.

Nos falta más información.
We lack/need more information

124 Es de ... ('it's to be ...')
No es de ... ('it's not to be ...')

These expressions are followed by the infinitive in Spanish.

Examples:

es de esperar.
it is to be expected.

una ocasión que no era de perder
an opportunity which was not to be missed

Comprehension Practice 11

Look at the dialogue again and then answer the questions below:

New words:

la prioridad	priority
servir para	to be used for

1 ¿Dónde y cuándo tendrá lugar la feria?
2 ¿Cuáles de sus nuevos productos quiere promover Marketofisa?
3 ¿Qué hizo Guillermo el año pasado?
4 Según Guillermo, ¿cuál es la prioridad?
5 ¿Por qué intenta conseguir un buen sitio?
6 ¿Qué facilidades quieren ofrecer a sus visitantes?
7 ¿Para qué serviría una sala en el stand?
8 ¿En qué está trabajando el departamento de Márketing?
9 ¿Por qué cree Peter que no van a tener problemas en formar un equipo para ir a Méjico?
10 ¿Quién se encarga de organizar el alojamiento?
11 ¿Quién pagará los costes del transporte de los equipos?
12 ¿Cómo eran las facilidades de la exposición el año pasado?
13 ¿Por qué no llama Guillermo en seguida a Méjico?
14 ¿Qué va a hacer Guillermo en cuanto reciba una contestación?

FLUENCY PRACTICE 57

New words:

el/la estudiante	student
la película	film
practicar	to practise
el deporte	sport
jugar al tenis	to play tennis (stem-changing u → ue)
coger	to take (transport) (Peninsular Spanish)
tomar*	to take (transport) (Mexican Spanish)
el carro	car (Mexican Spanish)

(*NOTE: Mexicans would not use the verb **coger** since its only meaning is indecent. On the other hand, in Spain its use is commonplace and quite acceptable)

Answer the following questions using the imperfect tense. Here are two examples:

¿Vas mucho al cine?
Do you go to the cinema a lot?
(was student/went a lot)

Ahora no, pero cuando era estudiante, iba mucho.
Not now, but when I was (a) student, I went/used to go a lot.

¿Veis mucho a vuestros abuelos?
Do you see much of your grandparents?
(lived in England/saw them once a week)

Ahora no, pero cuando vivíamos en Inglaterra, les veíamos una vez a la semana.
Not now, but when we lived in England, we saw/used to see them once a week.

1 ¿Vas mucho al cine? (was younger/saw a film every Saturday)
2 ¿Vais al trabajo en coche? (lived on the outskirts/took the car)
3 ¿Vives en un piso? (studied in Barcelona/had one in the centre)
4 ¿Viajas mucho al extranjero? (was sales manager/travelled a lot in Europe)
5 ¿Practicas algún deporte? (was 20 years old/played tennis)
6 ¿Salís mucho por las noches? (were students in Madrid/went out every night)
7 ¿Ganas mucho dinero? (worked in USA/earned more)

FLUENCY PRACTICE 58

Imagine you are Peter Jackson in your new job in Spain. Answer the following questions which his Spanish colleagues put to him:

1 ¿Dónde vivías?
2 ¿Cómo se llamaba tu empresa?
3 ¿Qué puesto ocupabas?
4 ¿Cuántas personas tenías en tu equipo?
5 ¿Te gustaba el trabajo?

FLUENCY PRACTICE 59

New words:

el hospital	hospital
dormirse	to fall asleep
la pastilla	pill

Change the verb in the brackets either using the subjunctive or the indicative. Look back at Checknotes 112 and 119 to remind yourself of the rules:

1 Llamó a su madre en cuanto (**llegar**) a casa.
2 Bajarán a la recepción después de que (**terminar**) la entrevista.
3 Vamos a hablar con el director tan pronto como (**él volver**) del congreso.
4 Fuimos al hospital en cuanto (**oír**) lo que pasó.
5 Mandará el resto tan pronto como (**confirmarse**) la reservación.
6 Empezó a escribir la respuesta tan pronto como (**recibir**) la carta.
7 En cuanto (**tomar**) las pastillas, se dormirá.

FLUENCY PRACTICE 60

New words:

el minuto	minute
la mesa	table
quedarse	to stay

Respond as directed to the following questions or comments. Use a preposition and the appropriate personal pronoun.

Example:

¿Vas a echar las cartas ahora?
Are you going to post the letters now?

Sí, las tengo conmigo.
Yes, I have them with me.

1 ¿Hiciste la reserva?
   [Yes, I booked a table for you for nine o'clock. (use **tú**)]
2 ¿Tienes el libro?
   [Oh, no. I've come without it.]
3 ¿Trabaja contigo?
   [No, no, he works with them.]
4 Debo mandar una contestación.
   [Don't worry, I've already written for you.]
5 ¿Quiénes van a estar en la entrevista?
   [Besides you and Mr López, I don't know.]
6 ¿Cuándo llegaron mis padres?
   [A few minutes after you. (use **vosotros**)]
7 ¡Juan! ¡Enrique! ¿venís conmigo?
   [No, they've decided to go with us.]

ADDITIONAL PRACTICE

Finally, see if you can understand the dialogue recorded on cassette.

KEY TO EXERCISES

UNIT 1

Comprehension Practice 1
1 V, 2 F, 3 V, 4 F, 5 F, 6 F

Fluency Practice 1
Buenos días, tengo una cita con la señorita Martín.
De parte del/de la ...
Gracias

Buenas tardes, tengo una cita con la señora Martín.
De parte del/de la ... de la compañía norteamericana Equip.
Gracias.

Fluency Practice 2
está en   estoy en   estamos en   están en
están en   está en

Fluency Practice 3
los señores, unos despachos, las señoritas italianas
Tenemos unas citas.
Las compañías tienen unas recepcionistas británicas.

Fluency Practice 4
Tiene una cita.
Tengo un despacho en la cuarta planta.
La recepcionista tiene mi tarjeta.
Tienes una secretaria italiana.
Tenemos una compañía en Nueva York.

UNIT 2

Comprehension Practice 2
1 V, 2 F, 3 F, 4 F, 5 F, 6 V, 7 F, 8 F

Fluency Practice 5
1 ... esperar en la recepción, por favor?
2 ... pasar el día en Madrid?
3 ... representar a la compañía en la reunión?
4 ... tomar una cerveza?
5 ... organizar la cita con la señorita López?
6 ... reservar el hotel?

Fluency Practice 6
1 . . . tomar una cerveza.
2 . . . estar en Madrid a las siete.
3 . . . pasar diez días en Barcelona.
4 . . . hablar enseguida con el señor González.
5 . . . esperar en la recepción.
6 . . . representar a la compañía británica en Zaragoza.

Fluency Practice 7
– ¡Hola! Buenas tardes. Soy Tom Smith. Tengo una cita con el señor González a las cinco.
– Sí, aquí tiene.
– Encantado de conocerle.
– Sí, un café, gracias.
– Sí, y también represento a dos compañías americanas. Somos especialistas en la ofimática.
– Gracias.

Fluency Practice 8
1 siete despachos
2 tres secretarias italianas
3 seis cafés
4 cuatro plantas
5 nueve días
6 cinco compañías británicas
7 ocho hoteles
8 quince especialistas
9 veintinueve bares
10 un té
11 veinte citas
12 veintidós viajes
13 once cervezas
14 diecinueve tarjetas

Fluency Practice 9
1 estoy 2 es 3 estamos 4 estar 5 son 6 Son 7 es
8 Son 9 estáis 10 son

Fluency Practice 10
1 represento 2 espera 3 pasamos 4 organiza 5 tomamos
6 voy a pasar 7 hablan 8 baja 9 reserváis 10 acompañan

UNIT 3

Comprehension Practice 3
1 F, 2 F, 3 V, 4 F, 5 V, 6 F, 7 F

Fluency Practice 11
Nos especializamos en ...
a) ... la formación de personal.
b) ... tecnología avanzada.
c) ... la fabricación de máquinas de escribir electrónicas.
d) ... la ofimática.
e) ... la importación de ordenadores americanos.

Fluency Practice 12
1 Sí, importamos ....
2 Sí, escribe ....
3 Sí, trabajamos ....
4 Sí, vivimos ....
5 Sí, comen ....

Fluency Practice 13
1 No, no llevamos muchos años especializándonos en la ofimática.
2 No, su compañía no importa productos australianos.
3 No, nuestro cliente no está buscando a un representante.
4 No, no fabrica todo lo que se necesita para la oficina moderna.
5 No, el Mercado Unico no ofrece muchas ventajas.

Fluency Practice 14
a) Ella quiere   i) asistir al congreso.
b) Estoy   j) escribiendo una carta.
c) Vosotros   f) recibís el paquete.
d) La reunión   h) termina a las cinco.
e) La señorita Martín y el señor Smith   g) hablan en español.

Fluency Practice 15
a) bebo   b) terminamos   c) se llama   d) habla   e) vendéis

Fluency Practice 16
No. Ya exportamos ordenadores a Alemania. Creemos que hay/existe un mercado potencial para nuestros productos en España.

Nuestras fábricas en Inglaterra fabrican máquinas de escribir electrónicas. Por otra parte, su compañía se especializa en equipos de oficina, ¿verdad?

Observo que son especialistas en este campo. Esto es lo que estamos buscando.

Fluency Practice 17
a) Ellos llevan una hora hablando con el director.
b) Vosotros lleváis dos días esperando la carta.
c) Llevo media hora escribiendo el informe.
d) Llevas diez años trabajando en Nueva York.
e) Lleva seis años vendiendo equipos de oficina.

UNIT 4

Comprehension Practice 4
1 España representa un nuevo mercado para Excel-Equip.
2 Acaba de abrir una oficina en Alemania.
3 No, se encuentra en las afueras de París.
4 Va a trasladarse a las afueras de Francfort al final de este año.
5 Son muy altos.
6 Tienen problemas de contaminación, tráfico y alquileres muy altos.

Fluency Practice 18
Mi colega sí, pero . . .
a) yo vuelvo a las diez.
b) yo prefiero trabajar en Barcelona.
c) yo me refiero a la carta.
d) yo puedo empezar a las ocho.
e) yo pienso importar equipos de Francia.

Fluency Practice 19
a) queremos exportar ordenadores a Italia.
b) vamos a abrir una nueva oficina al final del año.
c) llevamos un par de años exportando a Alemania.
d) invertimos en Alemania y Francia.
e) pensamos establecernos en Málaga.
f) cerramos la oficina a las siete.

Fluency Practice 20
¿Ah, sí . . .?
a) mi oficina es más moderna.
b) mis productos son mejores.
c) exporto más ordenadores a España.
e) mi personal trabaja más.
f) Mi empresa tiene menos problemas.

Fluency Practice 21
Sí, a pesar de las dificultades, creemos que es el momento oportuno para probar el mercado español.

Bueno . . . los alquileres en Madrid son más altos que en Valladolid. Es una ciudad más pequeña, el transporte público es bueno y tiene menos contaminación. Creemos que la gente prefiere trabajar y vivir allí.

Oh, gracias. Nuestro director acaba de llegar hoy y pensamos ir a Valladolid mañana.

Fluency Practice 22
a) El director acaba de empezar la reunión.
b) Acabamos de leer el informe.
c) Los señores González acaban de levantarse.
d) Aquel hombre acaba de volver de Nueva York.
e) Acabo de llamarte.

Fluency Practice 23
Sí, ...
a) lo leo.
b) le buscamos.
c) estoy ayudándola/La estoy ayudando.
d) queremos explicarlo.
e) lo prefiero.

Fluency Practice 24
No puedo ....
a) debo escribir una carta al director.
b) debo asistir a una reunión en Alcobendas.
c) debo esperar a la señorita Martín.
d) debo volver al hotel enseguida.
e) debo explicar los aspectos principales del informe al director.

UNIT 5

Comprehension Practice 5
1 Tiene una excelente reputación.
2 Son muy competitivos.
3 Es muy complicado.
4 Dan por hecho que existen diferencias entre España y otros países europeos.
5 Ha hecho frente a la competencia de otras naciones desarrolladas.
6 Se ha desarrollado rápidamente.
7 Sí, están experimentando problemas económicos.
8 Se dirige al mercado europeo.
9 Quiere mejorar sus tasas de crecimiento.
10 Le da la oportunidad que ha estado esperando.

Fluency Practice 25
a) Ya las he escrito.
b) Ya lo he realizado.
c) Ya la he terminado.
d) Ya la he convocado.
e) Ya las he abierto.

Fluency Practice 26
a) Nosotros también estamos especializándonos en equipos electrónicos.
b) Nosotros también estamos dirigiéndonos al mercado español.
c) Nosotros también estamos haciéndonos muy competitivos.
d) Nosotros también estamos trasladándonos a las afueras.
e) Nosotros también estamos manteniéndonos en una línea favorable.

Fluency Practice 27
a) He abierto la oficina a las ocho pero no he llamado a Ecofisa en Alcobendas.

b) He explicado las dificultades a la señorita Martín, pero no he escrito el informe.

c) He asistido a la reunión a la una, pero no he convocado otra reunión con los representantes.

d) He comido con Juan en el bar pero no he solucionado los problemas con la recepcionista.

e) He empezado el estudio de mercado, pero no he terminado el informe económico.

Fluency Practice 28
–Como ya le he comentado, los resultados de nuestro estudio de mercado nos hacen pensar que nuestros productos pueden tener éxito en España.

–Bueno, yo soy muy optimista, y creo que el Mercado Único nos ha dado una oportunidad excelente para ampliar nuestra área de ventas.

–Si, siempre hay que tener cuidado en un mercado muy competitivo, pero podemos asegurarle que tanto nuestra compañía como nuestras máquinas tienen una buena reputación.

Fluency Practice 29
a) Fabricamos tanto máquinas electrónicas como automatizadas.
b) Exportamos equipos tanto a Holanda como a Bélgica.
c) Tenemos en cuenta tanto los problemas como las ventajas.
d) Hemos considerado la posibilidad de establecer una oficina tanto en el centro como en las afueras.
e) Nos referimos tanto al estudio de mercado como al informe económico.

Fluency Practice 30
a) Los problemas se han hecho cada vez más difíciles.
b) Los resultados han sido cada vez más favorables.
c) Nuestras tasas de crecimiento se han mejorado cada vez más rápidamente.
d) El Mercado Único ha dado cada vez más oportunidades.
e) Nuestras ventas se han aumentado cada vez más rápidamente.
f) La economía se ha mantenido en una línea cada vez menos favorable.
g) Los precios se han hecho cada vez menos competitivos.
h) Los alquileres se han hecho cada vez menos económicos.
i) La compañía se ha desarrollado cada vez menos rápidamente.
j) Nuestra compañía ha exportado cada vez menos máquinas a Europa.

UNIT 6

Comprehension Practice 6
1 Comparten la misma opinión.
2 No se han producido muchos cambios en el mercado de la ofimática.
3 Han tendido a comprar productos japoneses o americanos.
4 Están financiando el programa de expansión.
5 Son muy conservadores.
6 Esperan tasas de inflación muy elevadas.

7 Son inferiores o equivalentes a los de Gran Bretaña.
8 Tendrá que buscar nuevas fuentes de suministro.
9 Estará dispuesta a incorporar equipos británicos a su gama de productos.
10 Va a enseñarle sus folletos.

Fluency Practice 31
1 No, lo terminaré mañana.
2 No, lo haré mañana.
3 No, podremos asistir mañana.
4 No, la abriré mañana.
5 No, la cambiaré mañana.
6 No, la veremos mañana.
7 No, la tendrá mañana.
8 No, se mejorará mañana.
9 No, bajará mañana.
10 No, lo solucionarán mañana.

Fluency Practice 32
1 Es el peor que hemos experimentado.
2 Es la mejor que hemos probado.
3 Son los más favorables que hemos tenido.
4 Son los más avanzados que hemos vendido.
5 Es el más difícil que hemos hecho.

Fluency Practice 33
1 Ya se lo he enseñado.
2 Ya se la he explicado
3 Ya se la he pedido.
4 Ya os los he dado.
5 Ya te la he leído.

Fluency Practice 34
1 Los resultados no han sido tan favorables este año.
2 ¡Es tan optimista!
3 ¿Podremos solucionar un problema tan complicado?
4 Hay tanto tráfico en la ciudad hoy día.
5 Hemos experimentado tantas dificultades.

Fluency Practice 35
1 Los que importan Vds. son alemanes.
2 El que utilizan Vds. es más flexible.
3 Las que tienen Vds. están en el centro.
4 Los que buscan Vds. tienen que ser modernos y atractivos.
5 Los que compran Vds. se han desarrollado en los Estados Unidos.

Fluency Practice 36
1 Los clientes tienden a comprar equipos franceses.
2 Los franceses tratan de penetrar en el mercado.

3 Las compañías tienen que/deben buscar nuevas fuentes de suministro.
4 Nuestros competidores tardan en introducir sistemas flexibles.
5 Los costes van a ser inferiores.

Dictionary Practice 1

SUMMARY

Letter from Peter Jackson (Sales Manager, Excel-Equip) to Srta Martín (Sales Director, Ecofisa) dated 21st April 199-.

Thanks for your letter of 16th agreeing to represent Excel-Equip and market our products in Spain.

I now confirm the main points of our discussions:

commission of 25% on all sales
to include all advertising expenses and participation in Spanish trade fairs

advertising campaign
inform Excel-Equip of possibility

delivery of goods
by lorry direct to your Alcobendas warehouse, free of charges, within a period of three to four weeks following receipt of order

payment of invoices
by bank transfer to our bank (NatWest, Regent Street, London W1) every two months, after deduction of commission

Excel-Equip to receive monthly sales report

Excel-Equip to send bi-lingual technician to arrange a training course to support after-sales service

I look forward to successful collaboration between our two companies. Yours sincerely, Peter Jackson.

Fluency Practice 37
1 Agradecemos su carta.
2 Me complace confirmar ...
3 Se incluirán todos los gastos.
4 la entrega de los bienes.
5 El pago de las facturas se realizará a través de transferencia bancaria.
6 Quisiéramos recibir un informe de ventas mensual.
7 Vds. se encargarán del servicio postventa.
8 Pondremos a su disposición ...
9 Un técnico podrá organizar un curso de instrucción.
10 Estamos seguros de que la colaboración entre nuestras compañías será muy fructífera.

Fluency Practice 38
1 on 11th April.
2 latest catalogue and price list.
3 electronic equipment.
4 more details about typewriters.
5 can he pay by bank transfer and can they make immediate deliveries.

Fluency Practice 39
Muy señores míos:
Acabo de recibir su carta fechada el 12 de abril en la que adjunta un folleto informativo de sus productos.
Me interesan especialmente los contestadores automáticos y les ruego enviarme más detalles sobre el contestador 'Elegante'.
Quisiera saber si Vds. ofrecen un servicio de postventa y si pueden efectuar entregas inmediatas.
Les saluda atentamente,

UNIT 7

Comprehension Practice 7
1 F, 2 F, 3 V, 4 F, 5 F, 6 V, 7 V, 8 F, 9 V, 10 V.

Fluency Practice 40
1 Es mejor que las pases en España.
2 Es importante que vayas cuanto antes.
3 Es importante que vuelva ahora.
4 Es mejor que estéis allí el viernes.
5 Es más importante que exporte a los países asiáticos.

Fluency Practice 41
Vaya al banco y ingrese estos cheques.
Eche esta carta; mándela certificada.
Cómpreme unos bocadillos en el bar.
Llame al Hotel Continental en Madrid y resérveme una habitación para mañana.
Escriba un fax a la señorita Martín informándola de mi visita.
Prepare estos informes para la reunión
No las distribuya hasta que las haya visto.
Acompañe a la señora López a la recepción y organice la reunión con el señor González.
Suba a la cuarta planta y entregue estos documentos.
Eso es todo, Gracias. Ah, y no tarde. Tenemos mucho trabajo.

Fluency Practice 42
- Buenos días. Soy John Cartwright, director de ventas de la empresa británica Euroquip. ¿Puedo hablar con la señora Redondo, por favor?
- Sí, por favor. Tengo una cita con la señora Redondo para el próximo miércoles a las tres y media, pero desgraciadamente he tenido que cambiar mi vuelo y ahora no llegaré a Madrid hasta las cuatro. ¿Será posible ver a la señora Redondo el jueves por la mañana?
- Sí, de acuerdo. ¿A qué hora?
- Perdone, no le oigo muy bien, ¿a qué hora?
- Sí, está bien. Gracias.
- No, no, es Cartwright, C-A-R-T-W-R-I-G-H-T.
- Adiós y gracias.

Fluency Practice 43
1 es 2 ser 3 está 4 es 5 son 6 está 7 somos 8 estar
9 esté 10 son

Fluency Practice 44
1 por 2 para 3 para 4 por 5 por 6 para 7 por 8 por
9 para 10 por

Fluency Practice 45
876543 ECOFISA M 345678 EXEQUIP L
TLX. 88889 27.09.93 15.00 ATN: SR. FRANCISCO GARCIA
REF: ENVIO IMPRESORAS
GRACIAS POR SU TELEX. ME ALEGRO DE QUE LA TRADUCCION ESTE
BIEN. SIENTO QUE NO HAYAN RECIBIDO LAS IMPRESORAS. EL
PROBLEMA ES QUE LAS ADUANAS BRITANICAS ESTAN EN HUELGA.
LE ASEGURO QUE HACEMOS/ESTAMOS HACIENDO TODO LO QUE
PODEMOS PARA EFECTUAR LA ENTREGA. ESPERO TENER MEJORES
NOTICIAS MANANA. SALUDOS PETER JACKSON
876543 ECOFISA M 345678 EXEQUIP L

UNIT 8

Comprehension Practice 8
1 Se especializa en la tecnología y la ofimática.
2 Está en Madrid.
3 Busca un director de ventas.
4 Deben tener al menos ocho años (de experiencia) en ventas.
5 Deben tener conocimientos de inglés, español, y un tercer idioma/una
   tercera lengua.
6 Tiene mucha experiencia en los sectores de ventas, exportación e
   informática.
7 Es española.
8 Está trabajando desde el año 1984.
9 Habla español, inglés y alemán.
10 Le interesan las artes marciales, el paracaidismo y la música.

Fluency Practice 46
a) ochenta libras b) veintitrés dólares c) treinta y tres libras
d) cuarenta y siete mil pesetas e) quinientos tres dólares f) siete mil
novecientos pesos g) cuatrocientas cuarenta y ocho libras h) cien
dólares i) cincuenta y ocho mil setecientas pesetas j) treinta y cinco
mil ochocientos cuarenta y seis pesos k) dos mil cuatrocientas treinta y
siete pesetas l) trescientos setenta y un mil dólares m) sesenta mil
quinientas diez pesetas n) ciento setenta y una libras o) seiscientos
veintiséis dólares

Fluency Practice 47
1 es 2 tenga 3 sepa 4 pueda 5 goza

Fluency Practice 48
vayáis   cojan   hayan   empiece   veas

Fluency Practice 49
tendría, me gustaría, podríamos, no haría, sería, terminaría

Fluency Practice 50
1 el mismo problema,   2 un nuevo coche,   3 compañía grande
   4 sector agrícola,   5 un mal servicio,   6 tercera planta   7 unas
hermosas vistas   8 el pobre señor

Dictionary Practice 2
1. promotions director,   2. employment agency/directors selection,
3. food,   4. Board of Directors,   5. support and introduce business
ideas and initiatives , define and propose commercial targets and policies,
world-wide analysis of markets with a view to expanding customer base,
preparing new projects,   6. minimum 10 years in areas of Management,
Commerce or Promotion, Development of Business
Projects.   7. University degree and Master in Administration or
Business,   8. Complete command of English and knowledge of a third
European language essential,   9. experience and
qualifications,   10. send CV and photo to the agency, ref. on envelope

UNIT 9

Comprehension Practice 9
1 V,   2 F,   3 V,   4 F,   5 V,   6 F,   7 V,
8 V,   9 V,   10 F,   11 V,   12 F,   13 F,   14 F.

Fluency Practice 51
Pues, creo que el puesto corresponde exactamente a mis objetivos
profesionales y a mi experiencia en este campo. Además me interesa
especialmente la dimensión internacional de su compañía.

He podido adquirir la experiencia necesaria para establecer y desarrollar
relaciones con clientes extranjeros. He ampliado mis conocimientos en el
campo de la promoción de ventas, y ahora estoy acostumbrado a dirigir a
un equipo de vendedores profesionales.

Sé que hay diferencias en las condiciones y prácticas laborales en
comparación con las empresas británicas. Después de todo, trabajé más
de un año en una empresa catalana. Sin embargo, espero responder
positivamente a esos cambios y adaptarme sin problemas.

Están muy entusiasmados con la idea de vivir en España.

El aumento inicial de sueldo es modesto, pero el puesto ofrece
posibilidades de ascenso y así estoy dispuesto a considerar el asunto
a largo plazo. ¿Podría darme más detalles sobre el paquete de
beneficios?

Es un paquete muy atractivo.

Normalmente tendría que avisarles con dos meses de antelación.

Sí, tengo una pregunta. ¿Funciona un horario flexible en su compañía?

Fluency Practice 52
1 dejé 2 escribió 3 empecé 4 diste 5 terminaron
6 se levantó 7 decidisteis 8 exportó 9 llamó
10. analizó, escogió

Fluency Practice 53
1 ¿Por qué? 2 ¿A qué hora? 3 ¿Cuánto tiempo? 4 ¿Cuál?
5 ¿Cuándo? 6 ¿Dónde? 7 ¿Cómo? 8 ¿Qué?

UNIT 10

Comprehension Practice 10
1 ¿Ya tienen una idea del tipo de propiedad que quieren, de su ubicación y sobre todo de su precio?
2 Hicieron un recorrido por varias zonas.
3 Busca un chalet, preferiblemente no adosado, con 4 dormitorios, jardín y garaje.
4 Porque no es aficionado al bricolaje y tampoco tendrá tiempo.
5 Están dispuestos a pagar entre 30 y 35 millones de pesetas.
6 Prefieren el que da a la sierra y vale 34 millones.
7 No, van a pagar al contado.
8 Tienen que incluir los documentos necesarios y su pasaporte o carnet de identidad.
9 Perderán su depósito que se pagará como indemnización al vendedor.
10 No, tendrán que pagar un depósito inicial cuando firmen el contrato y el resto antes o en el momento de firmar la Escritura.
11 Hay los derechos del notario, los costes de inscribir la propiedad y el IVA.
12 Se paga un 6 por ciento.
13 Hay que pagar una contribución al Ayuntamiento para los servicios municipales, otra a la Comunidad de Vecinos si existe, y otros gastos como luz, gas y teléfno.
14 No. La contribución se calcula según el valor de la propiedad.
15 Van a preparar los documentos y los arreglos para el depósito, y el señor Jackson hablará con el banco.
16 La construcción de una autovía cerca de la casa.
17 Se comunicará con el abogado de los señores Jackson.

Fluency Practice 54
1 Terminé el mío ayer.
2 Hicimos las nuestras el viernes pasado.
3 Mis hijos fueron allí el invierno pasado.
4 María escribió la suya anoche.

5 Los señores Smith compraron uno allí hace dos años.
6 Me puse en contacto con ellos la semana pasada.
7 Tuve que cambiar doscientas sesenta libras esta mañana.

Fluency Practice 55
1 comprar   2 pague   3 pueda   4 tiene   5 llegó   6 haya   7 vayas

Fluency Practice 56
Buenos días. Quisiera información adicional sobre un chalet en la
urbanización Galapagar.

El adosado, con tres dormitorios, que da a la sierra. ¿Cuánto es?

¿De qué facilidades dispone la urbanización?

¿Está habitado el chalet?

¿Es posible ir a verlo hoy?

Me gusta mucho el chalet. Una vez que se haga la oferta, ¿cuáles son los
trámites normales?

¿Un Contrato de Compraventa? ¿Qué es exactamente?

Con dinero que he heredado de mis abuelos.

No. Ya se han transferido los fondos de Inglaterra. ¿Tengo que hacer un
pago inicial?

¿Y cuándo se paga el resto?

¿Cuánto tiempo se debe calcular entre la firma del Contrato y la de la
Escritura?

¿Qué ocurre si me retiro de la compra?

Además del precio del chalet, ¿qué gastos hay?

Vale. Creo que tengo toda la información que necesito por ahora. Tendré
que hablar con mi mujer antes de hacer una oferta. Puede que tenga unas
ideas muy diferentes. Cuando hayamos tomado una decisión, me
comunicaré con Vd.

Dictionary Practice 3
1 the house in La Moraleja – it has an office (despacho). *Note that the Vila
   Franca Castillo house has a* **cocina-office** *which is a pantry or utility
   room off the kitchen!*
2 the flat in the Salamanca district
3 the flat in Moncloa
4 the house in Vila Franca Castillo – big rooms, 220m^2 + big plot. It also
   has a storage room.
5 the house in Alcobendas – pool, and big garage
6 the house in Las Lomas Bosque – it's empty.
7 the house in La Moraleja – adosado = semi-detached
8 the flat in Vaguada district

UNIT 11

Comprehension Practice 11
1 Tendrá lugar en Méjico del nueve al quince de febrero.
2 Quiere promover su ordenador portátil plegable y el notebook.
3 Organizó la representación de una compañía en el mismo recinto en Méjico.
4 Tienen que reservar el stand.
5 Porque quieren llamar la atención y no pasar inadvertidos en un rincón.
6 Quieren tener un sitio donde los visitantes puedan probar los equipos.
7 Serviría para poder hablar tranquilamente con los clientes.
8 Está preparando unos diseños para el material publicitario.
9 Porque es una oportunidad que no es de despreciar.
10 Guillermo se encarga del alojamiento.
11 Marketofisa pagará estos costes.
12 Eran realmente estupendas.
13 Porque es todavía demasiado temprano.
14 Va a poner al día a Peter con respecto al stand.

Fluency Practice 57
Ahora no, pero cuando ...
1 era más joven, veía una película todos los sábados.
2 vivíamos en las afueras, cogíamos el coche/tomábamos el carro.
3 estudiaba en Barcelona, tenía uno en el centro.
4 era director de ventas, viajaba mucho en Europa.
5 tenía veinte años, jugaba al tenis.
6 éramos estudiantes en Madrid, salíamos todas las noches.
7 trabajaba en los EE.UU ganaba más.

Fluency Practice 58
1 Vivía cerca de Londres. 2 Se llamaba Excel-Equip. 3 Ocupaba el puesto de director de ventas. 4 Tenía doce personas en mi equipo 5 Sí, me gustaba mucho.

Fluency Practice 59
1 llegó 2 terminen/hayan terminado 3 vuelva 4 oímos 5 se confirme/se haya confirmado 6 recibió 7 tome/haya tomado

Fluency Practice 60
1 Sí, reservé una mesa para ti para las nueve.
2 Oh no, he venido sin él.
3 No, no, trabaja con ellos.
4 No te preocupes, ya he escrito por ti.
5 Además de ti y el señor López, no sé.
6 Unos (pocos) minutos después de vosotros.
7 No, han decidido ir con nosotros.

BUSINESS GLOSSARY

A

abroad
  go abroad ir al extranjero (*m.*)
  live abroad vivir en el extranjero
    (*m.*)
accept aceptar
account cuenta (*f.*)
  current account cuenta corriente
  deposit account cuenta de
    depósito
  open an account abrir una cuenta
accountant contable (*m.*)
acknowledge (receipt of) acusar
  recibo de
acquire adquirir
activity actividad (*f.*)
additional adicional
address dirección (*f.*)
advance
  in advance con antelación
advanced technology tecnología (*f.*)
  avanzada
advantage ventaja (*f.*)
  take advantage of aprovechar
advertisement anuncio (*m.*)
advertising publicidad (*f.*)
  advertising campaign campaña
    (*f.*) publicitaria
after-sales service servicio (*m.*)
  postventa
agenda orden (*m.*) del día
agent agente (*m.*)
agree estar de acuerdo
agreement acuerdo (*m.*)
  come to an agreement ponerse
    de acuerdo
agricultural agrícola (*m. & f.*)
allow permitir
American (norte)americano
amount importe (*m.*)
analyze analizar
annual anual

answering machine contestador
  (*m.*)
application solicitud (*f.*)
apply for solicitar
appointment cita (*f.*)
approximate aproximado
approximately más o menos,
  aproximadamente
area el área (*f.*), zona (*f.*)
arise surgir
arrange a meeting organizar una
  reunión (*f.*)
Asian asiático
atmosphere ambiente (*m.*)
attend asistir a
attention atención (*f.*)
  attract attention llamar la
    atención
automated automatizado
automatic automático
available disponible

B

balance saldo (*m.*)
credit balance saldo (*m.*) *acreedor*
debit balance saldo (*m.*) deudor
balance of payments balance (*m.*)
  de pagos
balance sheet balance (*m.*) de
  situación
bank banco (*m.*)
  savings bank caja (*f.*) de ahorros
bank draft giro (*m.*) bancario
bank statement estado (*m.*) de
  cuentas
bank transfer transferencia (*f.*)
  bancaria
bankruptcy quiebra (*f.*)
bear in mind tener en cuenta
Belgium Bélgica (*f.*)
belong pertenecer

benefit beneficio (*m.*)
better mejor
  get better mejorarse
bilingual bilingüe
bill cuenta (*f.*)
board of directors consejo (*m.*) de
  administración
  junta (*f.*) directiva
bonus bonificación (*f.*) paga (*f.*)
  extra
booking reserva (*f.*)
boss jefe (*m.*)
box caja (*f.*)
branch office sucursal (*f.*)
brand marca (*f.*)
briefcase cartera (*f.*)
bring about efectuar
British británico
brochure folleto (*m.*)
bureaucratic burocrático
business expenses gastos (*m. pl.*)
  comerciales
business studies estudios (*m. pl.*)
  empresariales
business trip viaje (*m.*) de negocios
buy comprar
buyer comprador (*m.*)

C

calculate calcular
calculator calculadora (*f.*)
call a meeting convocar una
  reunión
campaign campaña (*f.*)
Canada el Canadá (*m.*)
candidate candidato (*m.*)
capacity capacidad (*f.*)
card tarjeta (*f.*)
career carrera (*f.*)
careful
  be careful tener cuidado
carry out an opinion poll realizar un
  sondeo (*m.*) de opinión
cash dispensing machine cajero
  (*m.*) automático

cash desk caja (*f.*)
cash
  pay in cash pagar al contado
catalogue catálogo (*m.*)
Catalonian catalán, ana (*f.*)
certificate certificado (*m.*)
chain cadena (*f.*)
change cambiar
charge
  be in charge of encargarse de
check (over) the accounts revisar
  las cuentas (*f. pl.*)
cheque cheque (*m.*)
  traveller's cheque cheque de
  viaje
clarify aclarar
client cliente (*m.*)
client portfolio cartera (*f.*) de
  clientes
collaboration colaboración (*f.*)
colleague colega (*m. & f.*)
commission comisión (*f.*)
community comunidad (*f.*)
company compañía (*f.*) empresa
  (*f.*)
  parent company casa matriz (*f.*)
comparison
  in comparison to en comparación
  con
compensation indemnización (*f.*)
competition competencia (*f.*)
competitive competitivo
competitiveness competitividad (*f.*)
competitor competidor (*m.*) -ora (*f.*)
computer ordenador (*m.*)
computing informática (*f.*)
conclude concluir
conditions condiciones (*f. pl.*)
conference congreso (*m.*)
  conferencia (*f.*)
confirm confirmar
confront hacer frente a
conservative conservador (*m.*) -ora
  (*f.*)
consider considerar
consist of componerse de
construction construcción (*f.*)
consumer consumidor (*m.*) -ora (*f.*)

contact
  get in contact ponerse en
    contacto
contract contrato (*m.*)
contribute funds aportar fondos
corner the market acaparar el
  mercado
correspond corresponder
cost costar
cost coste (*m.*)
cost of living coste (*m.*) de vida
cost price precio (*m.*) de coste
Council of Europe Consejo (*m.*) de
  Europa
council services servicios (*m. pl.*)
  municipales
count on contar con
cover cubrir
curriculum vitae historial (*m.*)
  curriculum (*m.*) vitae
customer cliente (*m.*)
customs aduanas (*f. pl.*)

D

damage dañar
damaged dañado, deteriorado
damages daños (*m. pl.*) perjuicios
  (*m. pl.*)
data datos (*m. pl.*)
date fecha (*f.*)
decide decidir
decision
  make a decision tomar una
    decisión (*f.*)
decrease disminuir
deduct descontar
degree (univ.) licenciatura (*f.*)
delay retraso (*m.*)
delegate delegar
delivery entrega (*f.*)
demand exigir
department departamento (*m.*)
department store almacén (*m.*)
deposit depósito (*m.*)
design diseño (*m.*)
despatch envío (*m.*)

detail detallar
detail detalle (*m.*)
develop desarrollar
developed desarrollado
development desarrollo (*m.*)
diary agenda (*f.*)
display presentar
disposal disposición (*f.*)
distribute distribuir
document documento (*m.*)
dollar dólar (*m.*)
doubt duda (*f.*)

E

EC CE (*f.*)
EC regulations regulaciones (*f. pl.*)
  comunitarias
economic(al) económico
Economics Ciencias Económicas (*f.*
  pl.)
economy economía (*f.*)
efficiency eficacia (*f.*)
efficient eficaz
electronic electrónico
employee empleado (*m.*) empleada
  (*f.*)
employment empleo (*m.*)
enable permitir
enclose (in letter) adjuntar
England Inglaterra (*f.*)
English inglés
equipment equipos (*m. pl.*)
  piece of equipment equipo (*m.*)
equivalent equivalente
essential imprescindible
establish oneself establecerse
European europeo
European Community Comunidad
  Europea (*f.*)
European Union Unión (*f.*) Europea
examine examinar
exchange cambio (*m.*)
exchange rate tipo (*m.*) de cambio
executive ejecutivo (*m.*)
exhibit exponer
exhibition exposición (*f.*)

exhibition hall salón (*m.*)
expansion expansión (*f.*)
expect esperar
expense gasto (*m.*)
experience experimentar
experience experiencia (*f.*)
explain explicar
export exportar
extra extraordinario
Extremaduran extremeño

F

facility instalación (*f.*) facilidad (*f.*)
factory fábrica (*f.*)
facts datos (*m. pl.*)
faulty defectuoso
fax (tele) fax (*m.*)
fees (professional) derechos (*m. pl.*)
finance financiar
finances finanzas (*f. pl.*)
financial financiero
finish terminar, acabar
flexitime horario (*m.*) flexible
folder carpeta (*f.*)
forecast prever
foreign extranjero
formalities trámites (*m. pl.*)
fragile frágil
France Francia (*f.*)
French francés
frontier frontera (*f.*)
fruitful fructífero
fulfil one's obligations cumplir con sus obligaciones (*f. pl.*)
funds fondos (*m. pl.*)

G

gains ganancias (*f. pl.*)
German alemán
Germany Alemania (*f.*)
goods bienes (*m. pl.*)
Great Britain Gran Bretaña (*f.*)
greet saludar

growth crecimiento (*m.*)
growth rate tasa (*f.*) de crecimiento
guarantee garantía (*f.*)

H

hall sala (*f.*)
hand back devolver
handle
    easy to handle fácil de manejar
hard disk disco (*m.*) duro
hardware equipo (*m.*) informático
head office sede (*f.*)
help ayudar
help ayuda (*f.*)
Holland Holanda (*f.*)
hope esperar

I

import importación (*f.*)
import importar
importance importancia (*f.*)
important importante
improve mejorar
income renta (*f.*)
    income tax impuesto (*m.*) sobre la renta
incorporate incorporar
increase aumentar
increase aumento (*m.*), incremento (*m.*)
independent independiente
inflation inflación (*f.*)
inflation rate tasa (*f.*) de inflación
inflexibility inflexibilidad (*f.*)
inform informar
information información (*f.*)
inherit heredar
install instalar
insurance seguro (*m.*)
    take out insurance hacerse un seguro

insurance company compañía (f.)
de seguros
interest interesar
interest interés (m.)
interest rate tipo (m.) de interés
interview entrevista (f.)
interviewer entrevistador (m.) -ora (f.)
introduce presentar
invest invertir
investment inversión (f.)
invoice factura (f.)
Italian italiano

J

Japanese japonés
job puesto (m.) empleo (m.)
join a company ingresar en una
empresa
journey viaje (m.)

K

keep informed mantener al
corriente
keep up (one's) contacts with
mantenerse en contacto con

L

last durar
Latin America América (f.) Latina
Latin-American latinoamericano
launch lanzar
lawyer abogado (m.) abogada (f.)
layout presentación (f.)
leader líder (m., f.)
leadership liderazgo (m.)
lecture conferencia (f.)
letter carta (f.)
level nivel (m.)
lifestyle estilo (m.) de vida
loan préstamo (m.) crédito (m.)
local authority autoridad (f.) local
location ubicación (f.)
London Londres (m.)

lorry camión (m.)
lose perder

M

machine máquina (f.)
machinery maquinaria (f.)
main road autovía (f.)
make marca (f.)
manage a department dirigir un
departamento
management dirección (f.)
management review revisión (f.) de
la gestión (f.)
manager gerente (m., f.)
assistant manager subdirector
(m.) -ora (f.)
managing director director (m.) -ora
(f.) gerente
manufacture fabricar
manufacture fabricación (f.)
manufacturer fabricante (m.)
margin margen (m.)
market comercializar
market mercado (m.)
marketing márketing (m.),
mercadotecnia (f.)
materials material (m.)
matter cuestión (f.) asunto (m.)
maximum máximo (m.)
meeting reunión (f.)
memo nota (f.)
message recado (m.)
Mexican mexicano
minimum mínimo (m.)
model modelo (m.)
modernize modernizar
modification modificación (f.)
money dinero (m.)
monthly mensual
mortgage hipoteca (f.)
mortgage loan préstamo (m.)
hipotecario
motivate motivar
motivation motivación (f.)
move (to a place) trasladarse
municipal municipal

N

necessary necesario
need necesitar
new feature novedad (f.)
New York Nueva York (f.)
news noticias (f.)
newspaper periódico (m.)
notary notario (m.)
note observar, notar
notify avisar
number número (m.)

O

obligation obligación (f.)
observe observar
obtain obtener, conseguir
occasion ocasión (f.)
occasionally de vez en cuando
occupy ocupar
offer oferta (f.)
offer ofrecer
office despacho (m.) oficina (f.)
office automation ofimática (f.)
operate funcionar
opportunity oportunidad (f.) ocasión
   (f.)
opt for optar por
option opción (f.)
order pedido (m.)
   order-book cartera (f.) de
      pedidos
organize organizar
   get organized organizarse
organizer organizador (m.) -ora (f.)
outskirts alrededores (m. pl)
      afueras (f. pl.)
outweigh pesar más
overcome superar
owe deber
owner dueño (m.)

P

packaging embalaje (m.)

pamphlet folleto (m.)
parcel paquete (m.)
Paris París (m.)
participate participar
participation participación (f.)
party (in agreement) parte (f.)
pass (entry) pase (m.)
pay in ingresar
pay pagar
payment pago (m.)
   down payment pago inicial
pension pensión (f.)
percentage porcentaje (m.)
performance funcionamiento (m.)
period plazo (m.)
peseta peseta (f.)
peso (Mexican currency unit) peso
   (m.)
place sitio (m.)
plan proyecto (m.) plan (m.)
planning planificación (f.)
PO Box apartado (m.)
point punto (m.)
point of view punto (m.) de vista
Poland Polonia (f.)
portable portátil
portfolio cartera (f.)
position
   be in a position to estar en
      condiciones de
possible posible
   as soon as possible lo antes
      posible
post (job) puesto (m.)
post (a letter) echar (una carta)
Post Office Correos (m. pl.)
potential potencial
pound libra (f.)
practise practicar
preferable preferible
present actual
   at present actualmente
   at the present time en la
      actualidad (f.)
presentation presentación (f.)
price precio (m.)
   retail price precio (m.) al por
      menor

wholesale price precio (*m.*) al por mayor
principle principio (*m.*)
print imprimir
printer impresora (*f.*)
priority prioridad (*f.*)
private privado
problem problema (*m.*)
procedures trámites (*m. pl.*)
produce producir
product producto (*m.*)
production producción (*f.*)
productivity productividad (*f.*)
professional profesional
profits beneficios (*m. pl.*) ganancias (*f. pl.*)
programme programa (*m.*)
progress hacer progresos
promote a product promover un producto (*m.*)
promotion promoción (*f.*)
  get promoted ser promovido/ ascendido
property propiedad (*f.*)
proposal propuesta (*f.*)
propose proponerse
provide proporcionar, facilitar
public público
purchase compra (*f.*)

Q

quality calidad (*f.*)
quality (attribute) cualidad (*f.*)
query duda (*f.*)

R

range gama (*f.*)
rate
  exchange rate tipo (*m.*) de cambio

growth rate tasa (*f.*) de crecimiento
inflation rate tasa (*f.*) de inflación
interest rate tipo (*m.*) de interés
ready to dispuesto a
realize darse cuenta de
receipt recibo (*m.*)
receive recibir
recession recesión (*f.*)
recommend recomendar
refer referirse
reference referencia (*f.*)
register registrar, inscribir
registered (mail) certificado
regret sentir
remainder resto (*m.*)
rent alquilar
rent alquiler (*m.*)
reply contestación (*f.*)
reply contestar
report informe (*m.*)
represent representar
representative representante (*m., f.*)
reputation reputación (*f.*)
request rogar
requirement requisito (*m.*)
reserve reservar
residence residencia (*f.*)
  take up residence fijar residencia
resident vecino (*m.*)
residential development urbanización (*f.*)
residents' association comunidad (*f.*) de vecinos
resolve solucionar
respond responder
responsibility responsabilidad (*f.*)
result resultado (*m.*)
right
  be right tener razón
rise alza (*f.*) (*el.*)
risk
  take a risk arriesgarse

S

salary sueldo (*m.*)

sale venta (f.)
salesperson vendedor (m.) -ora (f.)
scale escala (f.)
searches investigaciones (f. pl.)
secretary secretaria (f.)
security seguridad (f.)
sell vender
send enviar, mandar
set in motion poner en marcha
share a flat compartir un piso (m.)
share the profits participar de los
  beneficios (m. pl.)
show mostrar
sign firmar
signature firma (f.)
signing firma (f.)
Single Market Mercado Único (m.)
situated
  be situated estar ubicado
size tamaño (m.)
solicitor abogado (m.) abogada (f.)
sort out the matter arreglar el
  asunto (m.)
source fuente (f.)
space espacio (m.)
Spain España (f.)
Spanish español
specialist especialista (m., f.)
specialize especializarse
specialized especializado
specific específico
spend (money) gastar
spend (time) pasar
stable estable
staff personal (m.)
stand out destacarse
stand stand (m.)
strike huelga (f.)
  be on strike estar en huelga
study estudio (m.)
subsidized subvencionado
success éxito (m.)
successful
  be successful tener éxito
suit (be convenient) convenir
suitable apropiado, adecuado
summarize resumir
supplier proveedor (m.)

supply suministro (m.)
support apoyo (m.)
sure seguro
  make sure of asegurarse de
surface area superficie (f.)
surname apellido (m.)
surroundings inmediaciones (f. pl.)
survey estudio (m.)

T

take place tener lugar
talk hablar
tariff tarifa (f.)
tax impuesto (m.) contribución (f.)
team equipo (m.)
technician técnico (m.) técnica (f.)
technology tecnología (f.)
telegram telegrama (m.)
telephone teléfono (m.)
terms of payment condiciones (f.
  pl.) de pago
test probar
test prueba (f.)
  put to the test poner a prueba
Thailand Tailandia (f.)
thank agradecer
theme tema (m.)
thoroughly a fondo
timetable horario (m.)
title deed(s) escritura (f.)
touch
  be/get in touch with comunicarse
  con
tour recorrido (m.)
town hall ayuntamiento (m.)
trade comerciar
trade comercio (m.)
trade fair feria (f.)
trade gap déficit (m.) comercial
trainee aprendiz (m.) aprendiza (f.)
training formación (f.) instrucción
  (f.)
transactions trámites (m. pl.)
transfer transferir
transfer (bank) transferencia (f.)
transfer (removal) traslado (m.)

translation traducción (*f.*)
translator traductor (*m.*) -ora (*f.*)
transport transporte (*m.*)
trial period período (*m.*) de prueba
trip
  go on a trip ir de viaje
turnover volumen (*m.*) de ventas
type tipo (*m.*)
typewriter máquina (*f.*) de escribir

U

unfortunately desafortunadamente
United Kingdom Reino Unido (*m.*)
United States, USA Estados Unidos
  (*m. pl.*) EE.UU.
unnoticed
  go unnoticed pasar inadvertido
up-to-date
  come/get up-to-date ponerse al
  día
urgent urgente
use utilizar,
  be of use servir
  make (good) use of aprovechar
used
  be used for servir para
  be used to estar acostumbrado a
useful útil

V

value valor (*m.*)
VAT IVA (*m.*)
vendor vendedor (*m.*) -ora (*f.*)
visitor visitante (*m., f.*)

W

wait for esperar
withdraw £50 retirar 50 libras
withdraw from an agreement
  retirarse de un acuerdo
word processor procesador (*m.*) de
  textos
work empleo (*m.*) trabajo (*m.*)
work trabajar, funcionar
working conditions condiciones (*f.
  pl.*) laborales
working life vida (*f.*) útil
workshop taller (*m.*)
worldwide mundial
worry
  be/get worried about
  preocuparse por
write escribir
written escrito

IMITATED PRONUNCIATION

UNIT 1

Recep.: ¡Bwáy-noss dée-ahss! ¿En kay pwáy-doh sairr-'béerr-lay?

Mr J.: ¡Bwáy-noss dée-ahss! Tén-goh óo-nah thée-tah kon lah sayn-yor-rée-tah Mahrr-téen.

Recep.: ¿Day páhrr-tay day kyenn, porr fah-bórr?

Mr J.: Del sayn-yórr Peter Jackson day lah kom-pahn-yée-ah bree-táh-nee-kah Excel-Equip. Ah-kée tyáy-nay mee tahrr-Háy-tah.

Recep.: Oon moh-mén-toh porr fah-bórr. ¿Kyáir-ray sayn-táhrr-say?

(*The receptionist phones through to señorita Martín's secretary.*)

Recep.: Sayn-yórr Jackson, lah say-kray-táhr-ryah day lah sayn-yor-rée-tah Mahrr-téen ess-táh kon oo-stéd en-say-gée-dah. Soo dess-páh-choh ess-táh en lah say-góon-dah pláhn-tah.

Mr J.: Móo-chahss gráh-thyahss.

UNIT 2

Mr J.: ¡Bwáy-noss dée-ahss!

Secy.: Ó-lah. ¡Bwáy-noss dée-ahss! Soy Mah-rrée-ah Ló-peth, lah say-kray-táhr-ryah day lah sayn-yor-rée-tah Mahrr-téen. ¿Ess oo-stéd el sayn-yórr Jackson?

Mr J.: See. Tén-goh óo-nah thée-tah kon lah sayn-yor-rée-tah Mahrr-téen ah lahss ón-thay.

Secy.: Ah, see. Lay ess-páir-rah en soo dess-páh-choh. ¿May ah-kom-páhn-yah, porr fah-bórr?

(*The secretary knocks on the door*).

Srta M.: See. Ah-day-láhn-tay.

Secy.: Sayn-yor-rée-tah Mahrr-téen, el sayn-yórr Jackson ess-táh ah-kée.

Srta M.: ¡Ah! ¿Son lahss ón-thay yah? ¡Byenn-bay-née-doh ah Mah-dréed, sayn-yórr Jackson.

233

Mr J.: Gráh-thyahss. En-kahn-táh-doh day koh-noh-tháirr-lah.

Srta M.: Syén-tay-say, porr fah-bórr. ¿Kyáir-ray toh-máhr áhl-goh?

Mr J.: Oon tay. Móo-chahss gráh-thyahss.

Srta M.: Porr fah-bórr, Mah-rrée-ah, oon tay páh-rah el sayn-yórr Jackson ee yo boy ah toh-máhrr oon kah-fáy. Bwáy-noh. ¿ee kay tahl soo byáh-Hay?

UNIT 3

Srta M.: Gráh-thyahss porr soo káhrr-tah en lah kay ess-plée-kahn soo een-ten-thyón day ess-porr-táhrr ay-kée-poss day o-fee-thée-nah ah Ess-páhn-yah.

Mr J.: See, yah ben-dáy-moss nwáy-stross proh-dóok-toss en Fráhn-thyah ee Ah-lay-máhn-yah ee ah-óh-rah kon lah pray-sén-thyah day Ess-páhn-yah en lah Oo-nyóhn. Ay-oo-roh-páy-ah ee lahss ben-táh-Hahss del Mairr-káh-doh Oo-nee-koh, kray-áy-moss kay eks-ée-sten bwáy-nahss o-porr-too-nee-dáh-dess en el mairr-káh-doh ess-pahn-yól.

Srta M.: Bwáy-noh sayn-yórr Jackson, dáy-boh day-théerr kay noh koh-nóth-koh soo kom-pahn-yée-ah. Say yáh-mah Excel-Equip, ¿Bairr-dáhd?

Mr J.: See. Noh sóh-moss óo-nah kom-pahn-yée-ah del tah-máhn-yoh day óo-nah mool-tee-náh-thyoh-nahl. Tay-náy-moss nwáy-strah sáy-day en Lón-dress ee fáh-bree-kahss en óh-trahss thyoo-dáh-dess del soor day Een-glah-táir-rah. Sóh-moss mwee koh-noh-thée-doss porr tóh-doh el Rráy-i-noh Oo-née-doh yah kay yay-báh-moss móo-choss áhn-yoss ess-pay-thyahl-ee-tháhn-doh-noss en ay-kée-poss ay-lek-tróh-nee-koss páh-rah o-fee-thée-nahss. Proh-doo-thée-moss kahl-koo-lah-dór-ress, mee-kroh-orr-den-ah-dór-ress, proh-thess-a-dór-ress day tést-oss, tairr-mee-náh-less day eem-pray-sór-rahss, máh-kee-nahss tay-lay-fákss, kon-test-ah-dór-ress ow-toh-máh-tee-koss, et-tháy-tay-rah. Ess day-théerr, fah-bree-káh-moss tóh-doh loh kay say nay-thay-sée-tah en óo-nah o-fee-thée-nah moh-dáirr-nah.

Srta M.: Ob-sáirr-boh kay son ess-pay-thyahl-ée-stahss en tek-noh-loh-Hée-ah ah-bahn-tháh-dah.

Mr J.: See, éss-oh ess. Porr óh-trah páhrr-tay, tén-goh en-ten-dée-doh kay soo kom-pahn-yée-ah ess-táh ess-pay-thyahl-ee-tháh-dah en lah rray-pray-sen-tah-thyóhn day em-práy-sahss ess-trahn-Háy-rahss kay trah-báh-Hahn en el káhm-poh day lah o-fee-máh-tee-kah. Ess-táh-moss boo-skáhn-doh ah oon ray-pray-sen-táhn-tay koh-mairr-thyáhl. Ess-tay ess el moh-tée-boh day mee bee-sée-tah ah Mah-dréed.

INDEX

The figures refer to Checknotes, NOT pages.